Fantasy
*Invention, Creativity, and Imagination
in Visual Communication*

Originally published by
Editori Laterza in 1977 as
Fantasia
Invenzione, creatività e immaginazione
nelle comunicazioni visive

Bruno Munari

FANTASY

INVENTORY PRESS

A military "fantasia" in London
Photo: Mario de Biasi.[1]

Is Eve's offering an apple to the snake a
case of fantasy or distraction or…?

WHAT ABOUT CREATIVITY?

A study on fantasy will seem to many an
impossible task.
For some, fantasy is caprice, oddity, extravagance.
For others it is fiction, that which is false, an
illusion, an imagining, a superstition.
For some peasants a fantasia is a folk dance;
for others a hallucination, a fixation, a whim.
It can be understood as a reverie, a phantasmagoria,
an inspiration, or a form of transport. For the
military, it is an occasional exercise to be performed
when the usual rigorous rulebook isn't in force.
Fantasy is also irregularity, aimless tinkering.
And if that weren't already enough, isn't invention
also fantasy? And isn't fantasy also invention?
How might we situate fantasy with respect
to imagination? Is a lie a fantasy, invention, or
imagination? But isn't imagination also fantasy?
And can't fantastic images also assume the form
of sounds? Musicians speak of sonic images,
sound objects. How does one invent a fish story,
an air-cooled engine, a new plastic?
It's a fact that our human faculties work together,
so it can be difficult to sort out how and when
they operate discretely. Yet were we to provide
some definitions (however provisional and specula-
tive) of each of these capabilities with the aim
of analyzing them and establishing whether there
are constants that make sense and can be codified,
we will have encouraged their dissemination and
recognition of their value.
I take on this challenge with my daily experience
in mind as someone who continuously relies
on these faculties in every professional endeavor.

Deals with everything that hasn't yet come into existence even if it couldn't have existed.

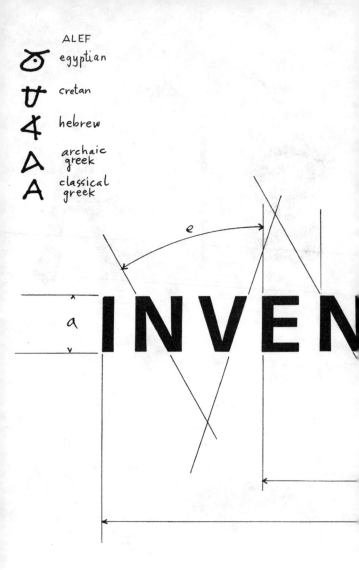

ALEF

egyptian

cretan

hebrew

archaic
greek

classical
greek

e

a

INVEN

Deals with everything that hasn't yet come into existence in the strictly practical realm, leaving aside all aesthetic questions.

11

CREAT

√ I ⌐ ⅄'

Deals with everything that hasn't yet
come into existence but is fully and
integrally feasible.

13

Fantasy, invention, creativity think;
imagination sees.

An instance of popular fantasy: fish and
birds flapping in the wind.

CONSTANTS

Who hasn't spotted a paint shop with a colorful
PAINT FOR SALE sign?[2] The words could be traced in
color gradients (like those of the rainbow) or each
letter painted in a different hue. A sign composed
of color blocks alone—of every color in the rainbow
on a palette or in a collection—might have been
preferable given that it would have worked perfectly
in Italy, India, China, Mexico…just about anywhere.
That's because that's the image someone looking for
a paint shop has in their mind. The words PAINT
FOR SALE add little.

I have cited this example to prompt the following
question: When it comes to signage, how come
paint shop owners everywhere in the world continue to favor color? One colors the word PAINT,
another colors the owner's name, another colors the
background for words written in black and white.
When it comes to paint shop signage there exists a
constant: a common mode of thought shared by the
majority of individuals.

People may believe that this solution is universally
intelligible. (There's some truth in this.) They may
believe that casting the wording in multiple colors
is ingenious. (There's no denying that the idea
makes sense.) The fact remains that many paint
shop owners adopt this type of signage because of
the direct association between the product and the
message being communicated to the public. It's
a question of coherence. The bicycle store hangs a
bicycle wheel over its door. The tire store displays
tires. The optician suspends a pair of oversize
glasses by the store entrance. And so on.

The logic that dictates the form that signage assumes is one and the same. It's a constant.

Might it be possible to study the constants of fantasy, invention, and creativity? Might it be possible to gain an understanding of how ideas are "born"?[3]

In the present book, I have sought to catalog and analyze what I view as the fundamental constants, the baseline cases, of this phenomenon. In so doing, I am well aware that I haven't exhausted the question of how fantasy, invention, and creativity operate. My aim is more modest: to clear the path for a more comprehensive, exhaustive study that will explain how one becomes a creative person.

The world of art, the worlds of creativity and fantasy, have always been maintained as a kind of secret preserve. Banish the thought of revealing how an idea is born or how an artwork germinates (presuming one knew the answers)! The public sees only finished works before which it stands dumbfounded. The Romantic artists in the midst of our avant-gardes insist that audiences must always be kept at arm's length, that artistic creation remains an ineffable mystery, that art collapses in the face of explanation. On the contrary, I believe that people genuinely wish to understand. As such, I have set about the work of explanation with the hope that others more competent than I will build upon these modest efforts to make sense of phenomena that interest everyone, with the hope of promoting the growth of creativity and personal development.

To embark on an exploration of this kind means tracing the entire process back to those faculties upon which cognition and memory depend. One must first attend to the ways in which intelligence operates with respect to the external (and internal) world, in order to then turn to the analysis of the rest.

THOUGHT THINKS AND IMAGINATION SEES

Our intelligence explores the external world by
means of logical manipulations and operations whose
aim is to understand the objects and phenomena
that surround us.
Sight, hearing, touch, and our other sensory receptors activate simultaneously, and intelligence seeks to
coordinate the flow of sensations in order to render
intelligible what is being experienced. That which
is understood is then registered in our memory
which is itself divided into three domains: short-term
memory, long-term memory, and genetic memory.
We store only that which is of immediate use value
in our short-term memory: I need to be at the
train station at 8 o'clock tomorrow. The thought is
preserved only until the moment I board the train;
then it is promptly forgotten. Our long-term memory
stores all of those forms of knowledge that help us
to lead better lives, to produce, to communicate,
to plan: all that is useful to us and sure to remain
useful. Information transmitted from parent to child
is stored in our genetic memory. Our memory is
supplemented by encyclopedias, inventories, archives,
and the like. Tables, diagrams, charts, etc. are
memory aids as well.
The memory of a child contains a limited amount
of information. The memory of an adult, quite a
bit of information.

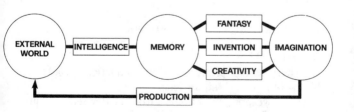

Intelligence at work

A thorn in nature (visual observation)
The sharp tip of a thorn pierces the skin (tactile observation)
All sharp things pierce the skin (deduction, proof)
Sharp objects can injure (elaboration)
A sharp weapon (invention): an object devised to injure

FANTASY
INVENTION
CREATIVITY
IMAGINATION

Fantasy is the freest faculty of all. It is uncon-
strained by that which is feasible or functional with
respect to its creations. It is free to think whatever
it wants, even to think the most absurd, implausible,
impossible things.

Invention makes use of the same technique. Like
fantasy it steps outside the known but in the pursuit
of a practical outcome. One invents a new motor,
a chemical formula, a material, an instrument, etc.
The inventor doesn't fret about the beauty of his
creation. All that matters is that the invention works
and is useful. There are exceptions, of course,
like the neoclassical steam engine found in Milan's
Museum of Science and Technology, which reflects
a useless worry—the sort of merger of art and
engineering that is considered wrong-headed today.[4]
In other cases the invention is "decorated" after the
fact, like the sewing machines of the Art Nouveau
period that artists draped in decorations of gold
and mother-of-pearl.

Something should perhaps also be said about invention and discovery. To invent is to create something that didn't exist before. To discover is to find something whose existence wasn't known. Accordingly, one can properly state that Galileo invented the telescope, thanks to which he discovered Jupiter and its moons.

Creativity, too, is an instrumental use of fantasy, of fantasy combined with invention, approached comprehensively. In the field of design, creativity is understood as a mode of problem solving: a mode that, though unfettered like fantasy and rigorous like invention, addresses all aspects of a question, not just the image (as does fantasy) nor just the function (as does invention) but also the psychological, social, economic, and human factors. Design can be spoken of as the shaping of an object, a symbol, an environment, a pedagogy, a planning methodology for addressing collective needs, etc.

Imagination is a means to visualize, render visible that which fantasy, invention, and creativity think up. In some individuals, its presence is negligible; in others, abundant; in others, it's more active than you might think.
Some individuals are completely lacking in imagination which is perhaps why there are professionals who can visualize for them that which fantasy, creativity, and imagination have dreamed up. The "visualizers" in public relations agencies are a case in point; they are designers whose job is to provide an initial sketch or model to help a client to see. Then there are model builders who craft full-size or scaled-down versions of objects or large constructions such as bridges or houses, according to the dictates of a designer. To do so doesn't require imagination, but allows them to experience the designer's thought process, animated by fantasy or invention or creativity.

Visualizing a project by means of a scale
model. The project in question is Bruno
Munari and the Gruppo Progettisti
Associati's proposal for Piazza Cavour
in Como, Italy (1975). The model was
executed in wood by Mauro Mauri at a
1:200 scale.

Realism, Impressionism, Futurism,
Surrealism, Cubism explained by means
of images. The same object, a tin fire
truck, has been photographed in a variety
of ways in order to provide a visual
account of the core principles that inform
the style of a given era.

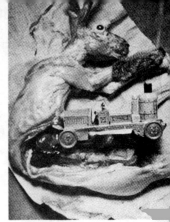

Realism sees the object as it is.
Impressionism sees it as incomplete,
requiring completion on the part of the
viewer. Futurism sees it in movement.
Surrealism sees it jarringly combined with
other objects. Cubism dissects it and
redistributes its parts along a single plane.

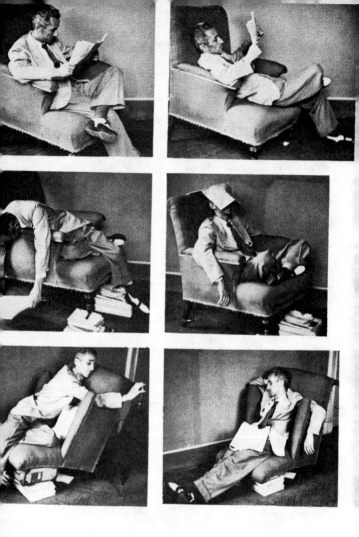

The visualization of a sequence of images documenting the pursuit of comfort in an uncomfortable chair.

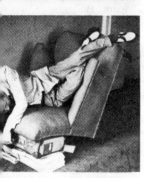

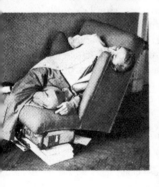

Imagination can thus be replaced by drawings, paintings, sculptures, models, films, kinetic artworks, and the like.

While fantasy, invention, and creativity give rise to something that heretofore didn't exist, the imagination can envision things that once existed but that have subsequently gone missing. It isn't necessarily a creative faculty. As a matter of fact, there are instances in which the imagination proves incapable of translating a fantasy into visual form. A case in point: imagine a motorcycle made out of wood. No problem! A motorcycle made out of glass wouldn't be hard to imagine either (not unlike those transparent models of the human body that expose all our inner organs). But what if we shift from solids to liquids and require a liquid motorcycle? No image comes to mind, no matter how vigorously one's imagination labors.

Think about all the people who see a face on the moon. Why only one face? Why not a peacock? Or a dung beetle? People haven't seen or memorized the image of a dung beetle, so they simply couldn't recognize it. While a human face is the very first thing that human beings experience as they enter the world. It's the first image committed to memory by all, so to see a face there is the simplest of associations. What do we see when we study the stains on a wall, marble fragments embedded in a pavement, stone formations, or clouds? Mostly faces. But there's always someone who sees a whale transformed into a camel.

> Hamlet: Do you see yonder cloud that's almost in shape of a camel?
> Polonius: By th' mass and 'tis, like a camel indeed.
> Hamlet: Methinks it is like a weasel.
> Polonius: It is back'd like a weasel.
> Hamlet: Or like a whale.
> Polonius: Very like a whale.
> —Shakespeare, Hamlet 3.2

THE CONNECTIONS BETWEEN
THINGS THAT ARE KNOWN

Fantasy's handiworks, like those of creativity and
invention, are born of perceived relations between
known things (the nature of these relations will
be elucidated later). It goes without saying that
it can't establish relations between two unknowns
or between something known and unknown.
You can't connect a pane of glass to *pfzws* but you
can, for instance, associate a pane of glass with
a rubber sheet. What is hatched when one imagines
such a connection? Perhaps an elastic form of
glass or a transparent rubber membrane. My imagination is activated in the process. Suddenly I can
envisage that stretchy glass.... What will happen
if I pull on it? Will it behave like glassy sheet of
water? My imagination begins to imagine it, to see
it. My creativity tries to put it to some practical
use. The inventor in me starts to think about the
chemical formula needed to manufacture it.

Accordingly, fantasy will be more or less vivid as a
function of the connections that a given individual
is capable of establishing. An individual with limited
cultural horizons can't develop an expansive aptitude
for fantasy. He must work with the tools he possesses
and with what he knows; knowing little, he can,
at best, imagine sheep covered in leaves instead of
in wool. That's already a suggestive leap. Instead
of establishing further connections, however, he will
be forced to stop thereafter.

Many believe that children are endowed with an exceptional aptitude for fantasy because their drawings and speech contain so many elements that surpass reality. Or they believe in children's exceptional powers because, conditioned and impeded by their life experience, adults feel incapable of making such things up. The truth is that, in this case as well as others, children are engaged in a simple operation: they project what they know onto what they don't. A child eats, cries, sleeps, chatters with its mom, poops, walks, and sleeps. Not knowing the world at large, the child imagines every object as participating in this world. The large ball is the mother of the baby ball. If soiled, the ball has pooped on itself. The ball feels cold or warm just like a child. And so on and so forth. This isn't fantasy; it's the projection of one's known world onto everything else.

If our aim is to ensure that a child becomes a creative person endowed with exceptional powers of fantasy (and not deprived of them, as are so many adults), we need to ensure that the child absorbs the maximum possible quantity of information. Only as such is a child able to perceive the greatest number of connections and resolve problems as they arise.

Monkeys, too, perform feats of fantasy. When a monkey sees a banana in its habitat beyond its reach and spots a wood box with which it has played on other occasions, it compares their relative heights. It adds the height of the box to its own height (which has already proven inadequate to seize the banana), steps on top of the box and grabs the banana. A person incapable of fantasy would have died of starvation.

An experiment was carried out with six hundred elementary school children in Italy and the Ticino in order to establish their actual understanding of a problem.

Varying in age between five and thirteen, they were asked to describe the inside of their bodies by means of drawings accompanied by explanations. The two organs that prevail in the resulting drawings are the heart and brain. The circulatory system is the system most often mentioned. The skeleton is less frequently mentioned except by the most mature kids. The digestive system is reduced to tubes connected to the mouth and apertures down below: children understand that when they ingest something through their mouths, organic matter will exit their bodies after a certain interval. Lungs tend to be placed randomly, as are bones. Children who frequent religious schools sometimes situate a little angel or devil within their bodies. The experiment was carried out with Italian and Swiss teachers by a group of psychologists from the University of Geneva. The team included Alberto Munari, Giusi Filippini, Mauro Regazzoni, and Anne-Sylvie Visseur (from *Archives de Psychologie*, Geneva).[5]

I don't know what's in the human body

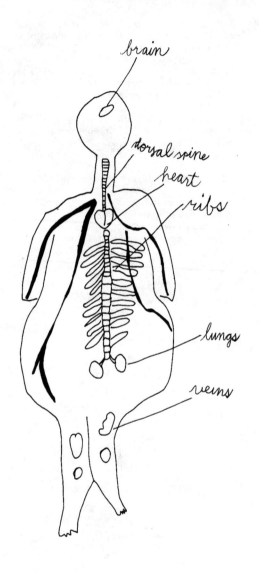

brain

dorsal spine

heart

ribs

lungs

veins

Fantasy is the faculty that permits the thinking of objects that have never existed. Fantasy is free to dream up completely imaginary, new, unprecedented objects but never worries about verifying whether they are truly new. That's not its job.

If we really want to know, that's a job for reason and for the gathering of the necessary data that will confirm whether or not the object already exists or is truly novel. An individual endowed with fantasy can dream up something that is new to that individual without any concern for whether it is truly unprecedented. Dreaming up new things is so pleasurable in itself that novelty for oneself is more than sufficient.

There were painters who "discovered" abstraction in 1976 after years of intense commitment to figurative painting: a disquieting innovation! Adopting this new mode of expression, they could well have found themselves repeating the experience of preceding generations of painters without even knowing it. When they exhibit these new works they will doubtless be told that abstractionism is hardly a novelty. The example of these artists is like so many other cases: they didn't bother to confirm whether theirs was a novelty only for them or an absolute novelty at the moment of decision.

There are, accordingly, two forms of novelty: novelty for the individual and absolute novelty. For an individual who ignores the artistic movements of the past half century, abstractionism is novel. It isn't novel for someone who is culturally attuned and aware of the dates of major breakthroughs and of their consequences.

We can conclude, therefore, that fantasy is free to dream up novelties of every variety. Only when the results are presented to an audience does it become necessary to verify whether the novelty in question is individual or absolute.

In fact, in the case of inventions, the patent system requires research into precedents before a patent can be granted.[6]

In order to understand the ways that fantasy, creativity, or invention function we need to study whether it is possible to identify the operations that take place in our memory with the knowledge we already possess.

It would seem that the most elementary exercise performed by fantasy is that of turning a situation on its head: to think the contrary, the opposite— "the world upside down" so to speak.

Next in line is repeating something without changes. Many instead of few. All identical or with variations.

Then there are visual or functional affinities: the leg of a table = the leg of an animal.

Next there is a group of associations that we could place under the umbrella of transformations or substitutions: changes in color, in weight, in material, in site, in function, in size, in motion...

Then there's the amalgamation of multiple hetero-geneous items into a single object as found in the visual arts, in drawing, paintings, sculptures, and films...like monsters and the like.

Lastly, there's the establishing of connections between connections: an object that is the contrary of another object found in an unexpected location, with a new material and in a new color...

This represents a first account of examples and connections (for subsequent development) with the aim of establishing whether it is possible to codify rules, to detect constants, to identify the data that can be applied in most cases. When it comes to developing a capacity for fantasy, the fundamental challenge is to increase one's knowledge base so that one can visualize a greater number of relations within that expanded set of facts. In no way does this imply that a highly educated individual must necessarily be endowed with a powerful sense of fantasy. On the contrary, there are people who pass for being highly intelligent only because they have memorized large quantities of information: an impression reducible to their powers of memory. They aren't really exercising their powers of fantasy if they don't see connections between the things that they know. They remain little more than a splendid warehouse of inert facts: not unlike a dictionary that contains all the words with which one composes poems but not a single actual poem. An idle instrument.

The time to expand one's knowledge base and to memorize information is, of course, childhood. The method of ingestion is play. Many of the world's designers have recently set about devising creative games, tools for stimulating the development of creativity and fantasy.[7] These new toys encourage children to act, to participate, to put their fantasies into practice by solving simple problems or visualizing multiple courses of action or building something in three-dimensional space out of modular components. A child who plays with such toys—think of LEGO or its equivalent—will find it easier to understand the challenges associated with prefabricated buildings than a child who has only played with a ball. It is during the early years of life that individuals assume the shape that they will retain during the rest of their lives. Whether they

Understanding a sequence of images means understanding the mutations they undergo. A pear isn't just a pear. It is also a moment in the transmutation of seed into seed by means of a tree, a flower, a fruit. To acquaint children with the mutability of things is to ensure that they develop a more flexible and capacious mindset. Designers have devised educational games to this end, valuable to children ranging in age from three to seven or eight years old. Photo: Jacqueline Vodoz.[8]

become creative or, instead, mere repeaters of existing codes depends on their teachers. Individuals either become free or conform to precedent during these formative years during which they accrue experiences and memorize facts. Adults must be mindful of this enormous responsibility: the future of society depends upon it. Fantasy, creativity, and invention continuously percolate within popular culture. Their enduring legacies form what is commonly referred to as a tradition, whether understood in the technical or artistic sense of the word. Traditions are continuously tested against subsequent acts of fantasy and creativity, leading to the substitution of elements that have become dated. As such, a tradition is the sum total of tenets, forever in flux, that people find useful. To unthinkingly repeat one such tenet without exercising your capacity for fantasy means interrupting a tradition, contributing to its death. So, a tradition is also the sum total of tenets accumulated by a collectivity required to perpetually renew itself and stave off decline.

Many strange things can be encountered in the natural world: a potato that looks just like Aunt Caroline, a flying fish, a heart-shaped stone, a root shaped like a human body, a flower with a mouth, a two-headed calf.... People imagine such oddities as if they were expressions of nature's fantasy when, in point of fact, they are exceptions that actually exist: not fantasies but, at most, invitations for us to fantasize.
Let's pursue our analysis by looking at the following case studies.

FRIGID FIRE
BOILING HOT ICE

The most fundamental expressions of fantasy are usually the result of situations that have been turned on their head: the play of contraries, opposites, complementarities. If he says "green," then I say "red." A well-known vintage print, entitled *The World Upside Down*, displays a horse straddling a rider, a landscape floating above the clouds, sheep herding a flock of humans, and other similar niceties.[9] Children chuckle when we tell them that sugar is bitter and are tickled pink when we read them the story of a turtle who moves as quickly as a bolt of lightning.

We know that for more than three millennia humans have committed pairs of opposites to memory: good and evil, light and darkness, cold and hot, and so forth. And Chinese cosmology has lent us the the celebrated yin-yang symbol: a symbol of unity in the form of a disk composed of two identical but opposing forms, one black and one white, one rotating in one direction, the other in the opposite direction. These elements embody the unstable balancing act that is life: the equilibrium that every individual needs to maintain by correcting for imbalances as they arise. A peasant who has spent his entire life surrounded by green will instinctively paint his house red (most do). An urbanite will seek a peaceful refuge from city traffic jams in the heart of nature. Someone who works with numbers all day will find solace in painting. All these balancing elements are the precise opposites of the source of imbalance.

In fact, it's only natural and spontaneous that when one thinks of an item, one also thinks of its opposite. Such pairings are obvious in my view. Everyone

René Magritte, *Empire of Light* (1950).
Night and day, simultaneously present in
a landscape.

knows that a comic character who is fat makes us laugh in the company of a thin counterpart. If the first is unnaturally fat and the second unnaturally skinny, there's even more laughter. If the fat one is short and the thin one tall, they will elicit laughter even without doing anything. A simple detail can add complexity: if the super-fat and super-short one is red and the super-thin and super-tall one is green, the play of contraries is further reinforced. For purposes of exaggeration, let's attribute a deep voice to the super-tall, skinny, green individual and a high-pitched voice to the other. By considering the question of the equilibrium of opposites, it becomes easy to understand how an individual living on the edge of a desert, with its vast, uniform, featureless landscape, feels the need to devise richly decorated interiors, dense in imagery, and abounding in the sorts of details that cause the eye to linger. Flowers, shapes, ornate geometrical structures in varied colors, distributed throughout the entire environment from the floors to the walls to the ceiling.

Another case study in the equilibrium of opposites are the Egyptian pyramids with their monumental, finite rational volumes which contrast with the infinite, uncharted surrounding space. Geometrical forms suggest strictly rational, human thoughts, in the face of the unknown and mutable.

A more recent case in point is Frank Lloyd Wright's famous house built atop a waterfall [Fallingwater] where the home's stationary geometries are perceived alongside water's organic and dynamic flow.

Closer to our time, Marcel Duchamp exhibited a urinal as a fountain. An object that was the recipient of jets of fluid now emits them by becoming a fountain.

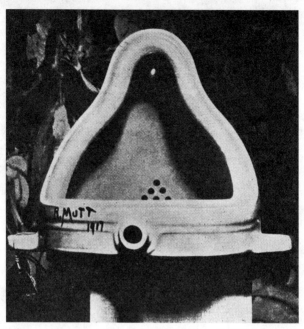

Marcel Duchamp, *Fountain* (1917). A urinal
exhibited as a fountain.

The vast and uniform desert landscape.
Photo: Mario de Biasi.

I myself observed this law of balancing opposites when I assigned the title *Useless Machines* to a series of kinetic objects devised in 1933.[10] A few years later, when I came up with my *Illegible Books*, I sought to experiment with every means of visual communication, to explore bookmaking methods that didn't rely upon words. I used the phrase "illegible books" because they were books without words. But, like a book, a visual reader can track their visual plot by studying sequences of colors, forms, and materials.[11] The books were made with papers of varying color and weight, with perforations whose continuation across multiple pages regularly shifts the visual context. Other books were made with two distinct colored papers, cut such that you can only turn a portion of the page but, as a result, you constantly rebalance the two colors. One of these books, thought up in 1949, made use of the sort of semitransparent paper employed by engineers; a red cotton thread stitched together the pages by loosely moving from one location to another. As you turned the page, the position of the thread changed. This book was published by the Museum of Modern Art in New York in 1967.[12] Another book with alternating white and red pages, variously sliced, was published by Steendrukkerij de Jong & Co in the Netherlands in 1953.[13]

Since antiquity, Asians have recognized that our bodies are mere extensions of nature and that man always lives under nature's influence…. In nature, there is order, a principle of constant flux, in harmony with the fundamental principle that our world is forever mutable.
—Naboru Muramoto[14]

The World Upside-Down, a popular
Spanish print.

Drawing: Fulvio Bianconi.[15]

Another fundamental feature of fantasy is the multiplication of parts within a whole that remains intact. A dragon with seven heads is perhaps the most famous case in point. Many Indian gods have multiple arms; others have multiple eyes or heads. Recently, the psychologist Edward de Bono carried out experiments regarding children's powers of fantasy, described in his book *Children Solve Problems*.[16] De Bono presented the children with a set of problems which he asked them to address by means of a drawing and a piece of writing. Among the prompts was: "improve the human body." The children were free to dream up any kind of solution. For them improving upon the human body meant modifying it in ways that would allow us to accomplish things we ordinarily can't. Among the most frequent solutions were ones involving the multiplication of single body parts. In the words of a nine-year-old girl who portrayed herself with six sets of arms: "I would like two additional pairs of arms to do things faster and touch stuff better. I'd want two in front and two in back. And I'd want five more fingers on each hand." This sort of multiplication of elements or parts of a whole doesn't modify the standard functions performed by what has been multiplied: many eyes are still employed for looking, many hands for grasping or touching. Often there isn't even a change in the dimensions involved in these elementary fantasies: the multiplied element retains the same scale as the original. In other cases, we encounter variations in size: the famous Russian stacking dolls [Matryoshka], lathe-turned and painted such that the smaller nests one within another that is slightly larger. Just like Chinese nesting boxes, graduated in size like the dolls. In such cases, fantasy has also relied upon another factor: the element of surprise.

We are unable to ascertain whether or how many other scaled replicas the object before our eyes contains. An avenue lined with identical, evenly spaced trees is another instance of a single element that has been multiplied by treating the avenue as a whole. This is an elementary use of fantasy; all the more so when the avenue with identical trees is flanked by buildings whose facades are all aligned. It would be much better to locate such an avenue out in the open countryside where one could travel down it flanked by highly varied trees, bushes, farms, gardens, houses, and animals. If anything, in an urban setting it would be preferable and more refined to develop avenues with varying trees: a linear composition that, instead of mirroring the monotony of the rest of the urban landscape, establishes a changeable linear garden composed of plants that flower at different times and of trees that are both evergreens and deciduous. Then you could say: come visit me at number 39 near the magnolia tree filled with birds.

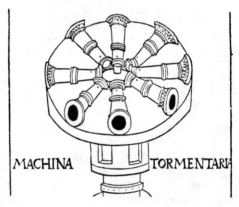

MACHINA TORMENTARIA

A *machina tormentaria* (rotating canon) designed around 1350. The platform supporting the eight canons rotates. A war machine of this kind creates the risk that a single spark may cause all eight cannons to fire at once.

An Indian god.

A single ballerina is potentially interesting,
two are more interesting; three, four,
five…even better. Twenty ballerinas
make a strong impression. Three hundred
ballerinas dressed identically personify an
industry, an assembly line, a Broadway-
branded mass production. They perform
exactly the same gestures, eat the same
hamburgers, drink the same drinks. The
one who asked for a beer was fired.

I'd like two more pairs of arms to use things faster and touch stuff better. I'd like two in front and two in back and two on the side. And I'd want five more fingers on each hand. And this is how I'd like my arms to bend backward: pushing a button that moves my arms forwards and back

Next page:
Roberto Lanterio, *Urban Reawakening*.[17]
Every individual in this drawing carries out the same operation in his cell. The multiplication of actions conveys the notion of simultaneous action on the part of individuals who all wake up at the same time in order to perform the same jobs. Only miniscule variations hint at their individuality.

54

55

A thing which once, myself, I chanced to view.
I saw come darting through a hedge,
Which fortified a rocky ledge,
A hydra's hundred heads; and in a trice
My blood was turning into ice.
But less the harm than terror...
—Jean de la Fontaine, "The Dragon with Many Heads
and the Dragon with Many Tails."

A cartoon by Searle.

A statue of Asura, the spirit of spirits, with three heads and six arms. A supernatural being who defeats her opponents with force and magic. A work by the Indian sculptor Mondōshi who was active during the Nara period in Japan (ca. 784 BCE).

An English cartoon from 1912 on Futurist art.

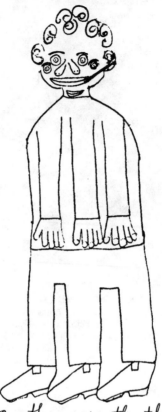

This is a boy these are the things that I'd like to have 4 ears 4 eyes 2 noses 2 mouths 3 hands and arms and 3 legs to get to school faster

Children's drawings that respond to the prompt: How to improve the human body. The children involved were seven, eight, and nine years of age. For additional examples, see Edward de Bono's *Children Solve Problems.*

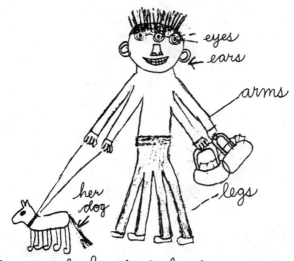

eyes

ears

arms

legs

her dog

she can do her food shopping all at once

The Procession of Virgins; Basilica of Sant'Apollinare in Classe, Ravenna.

Artemis of Ephesus, a symbol of the mother who feeds us all.

Constantin Brancusi, *Infinite Column* (1946).

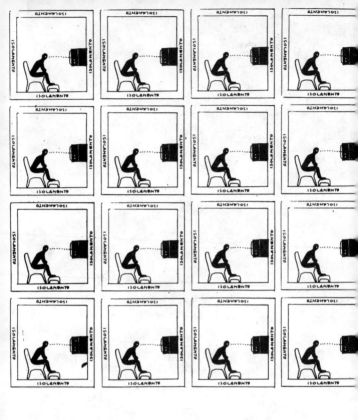

Isolation. Isolated from heat and from cold, isolated from the weather, isolated from the most pressing problems, isolated from nature, isolated from smells, isolated from friends, isolated from our peers...
Our only contact with the world is reduced to a unidirectional gaze. As such, individuals are flattened out and placed in the thrall of consumerism under the guise of ensuring safety and comfort.

A MONKEY WITH MUDGUARDS

Another facet of fantasy arises as a result of visual or other affinities. One day Picasso discovered that when viewed frontally, the body of a small toy automobile looked just like the snout of a monkey and set about creating a sculpture in which the toy appears as the monkey's snout. (Only a slight mental effort is necessary to rediscover the buried body of the toy car.)

The same artist portrayed the head of a bull in 1943 by combining a bicycle saddle and a set of racing handlebars on the basis of their visual affinities. Once hung on the wall, everyone perceived it as a trophy.

Famous are the portraits of Arcimboldo (1526–1593), assembled out of the strangest arrays of objects: fruit, fish, naked and leafy branches, mechanical parts. In the last of these, a set square becomes a nose, a clamp becomes a mouth, a spring becomes an ear, a gear becomes a head of hair…. Every object loses its meaning in order to assume a new meaning as a function of its use.

This specific instance of fantasy at work calls our attention to the fact that every object can be seen from a novel perspective. For instance, when looking at a standard fork, you can readily imagine it as a little hand endowed with fingers and a palm attached to a forearm extending up to an elbow. Once reimagined as such, procure yourself some malleable forks (the cheap ones) and, using a set of pliers, pose them in the full range of hand gestures. That's what I did in 1958 when I folded the "fingers" just right so that you could sense the underlying bone structure. There's even a fork for dieters in the form of a clenched fist.[18]

Have you ever seen one of those wide brushes with long bristles used by painters known as a *pennellessa*? If you look closely, you can readily imagine the bristles as a (perfectly well-combed) head of hair and add two little braids held tight by a small colored ribbon. You will then notice the femininity of the flat brush: the sinuous lines of the handle that evoke the sinuous contours of a female torso…the tin waist (or ferrule) held fast by little nails. From this moment on a flat brush ceases to be a tool for painting and is instead hung on the wall against the backdrop of violet-colored velvet.

The flat brush.[19]

Cartoon: Gerard Hoffnung.

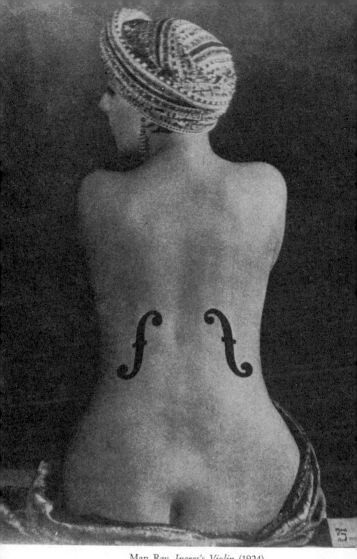

Man Ray, *Ingres's Violin* (1924).

THE BLUE BAGUETTE

Another facet of fantasy are changes in color.[20]
In 1960, Man Ray painted one of those meter-long
loaves of bread that are typical of Paris in cobalt
blue. The bread was still a loaf of bread but col-
oring it blue has rendered it inedible. Apparently,
there's nothing cobalt blue in nature that is edible.
The relation between color and edibility has been
the object of various experiments but no one
has ever been able to eat a blue risotto, no matter
how flavorful.
If you ask the first person who crosses your path:
so far as you are concerned, what color are extraterrestrials? The answer is sure to be "green." That's
because people imagine extraterrestrials as radically
unlike us—films and comics portray them as such:
so much so that their color must seem incredible.
As a result, people choose green because it is a
complementary color, which is to say the opposite,
of our rosy complexion.
Some circus clowns wear green wigs precisely for
this reason: to create an estranging effect, to make
children laugh.
Note that white is a color that can transform objects
into fakes. Try to imagine a bicycle, a coconut,
a typewriter, a ham...all painted in opaque white.
All fakes (even if accurate ones).

Man Ray, *Blue Bread* (1960).

Milton Glaser, *Portrait of Bob Dylan* (1966).
Milton Glaser states: In this portrait
I colored Dylan's hair in so many colors
inspired by Islamic art and remembering
the profile of Duchamp. Another instance
of shifts in color. For an everyday example
think of a brown-haired woman who dies
her hair blond.

A HAMMER MADE FROM CORK

Yet another facet of fantasy involves substitutions
of materials. There's a hammer entirely made from
cork (patented by Chaval) in Jacques Carleman's
Catalog of Fantastic Things specifically designed for
workers who work underwater.[21] In the 1950s there
were prank hammers for sale with balsa wood
handles and heads made from foam rubber instead
of iron. They looked exactly like hard and heavy
actual hammers but the minute you picked one up
you realized that it was light and soft: the perfect
instrument for (harmlessly) bonking someone on the
head. A boy to whom one of these lifelike, spongy
hammers was given went over to visit a friend one
day and, to play a joke on him, whacked him on the
head. Everyone laughed. Then another boy grabbed
his own hammer (a real one) and, to reciprocate,
whacked his little friend on the head. He started
crying and the party abruptly ended.
This same idea of switching materials is exemplified
by the famous Surrealist object created in 1936 by
Meret Oppenheim: a coffee cup with saucer and
spoon entirely covered in fur. Among the other
celebrated objects from this period of Surrealism are
the soft clocks painted by Salvador Dalí in 1931.
In 1944, Man Ray placed a flexible mirror on exhibit
that visitors could modify by pressing with a finger,
thereby distorting their own reflected images.
In 1963, [Claes] Oldenburg crafted a soft, empty
typewriter made from sheets of opaque plastic.
All the plaster models of cakes and ice cream
dishes exhibited in the display cases of coffeehouses
and pastry shops are yet another instance of the
substitution of materials even if they respect
the canons of realism.
The floppy umbrella used by circus clowns is a
normal umbrella minus its stays. When hung over

your arm it looks normal but when you open it up the whole thing sags. The invisible clothes described in the "Emperor's New Clothes" are another famous case involving the substitution of materials.[22]

There are cases of negative fantasy as well, typical of the nouveaux riches. When someone comes too easily into money and wants to provoke less fortunate friends, they can decide to substitute all the standard iron faucets in their home with gold-plated ones. This allows guests, as it were, to wrap their hands around their host's splashy spending habits. Of course, there will always be more cultured guests who will come up with ideas, unthinkable to those who think only about money, like installing faucets with photocell-activated automatic mixing valves.

> The moral of the fable is that those
> whose greed leads them to want
> everything, lose everything.
> I need no witness call
> But him whose thrifty hen,
> As by the fable we are told,
> Laid every day an egg of gold.
> "She hath a treasure in her body,"
> Bethinks the avaricious noddy.
> He kills and opens—vexed to find
> All things like hens of common kind.
> Thus spoil'd the source of all his riches,
> To misers he a lesson teaches.
> In these last changes of the moon,
> How often doth one see
> Men made as poor as he
> By force of getting rich too soon!
> —Jean de la Fontaine, *Fables*,
> "The Hen with the Golden Eggs."

Meret Oppenheim, *Untitled Object* (1936).

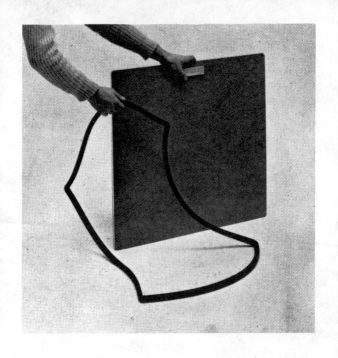

When a change in materials is creative in character it gives rise to a solution that, above and beyond aesthetic considerations, resolves a complex of issues. As a case in point consider the rubber frames for drawings, prints, and paintings developed by Munari for Danese. By substituting rigid framing materials for elastic ones, these frames overcome multiple drawbacks. There's no need to make use of nails when hanging them. Dust finds it harder to penetrate between the glass and the work of art. The frames absorb shocks when transported or dropped.

An instance of the erasure of materiality occurs instead in the 1933 film *The Invisible Man*.[23] The man in question had lost his materiality or, rather, his body has lost its visibility, due to a laboratory experiment with a drug. To regain his visibility, he is required to wear an overcoat, hat, shoes, and sunglasses, as well as swathing his entire head in bandages as if he were injured. His lack of materiality is staged by means of an extremely clever cinematographic trick: we see the invisible man standing in front of a mirror at home gradually unwrapping the bandages. Under the bandages we see nothing.

A scene from *The Invisible Man* (1933).

Salvador Dalí, *The Persistence of Memory*, 1931.

René Magritte, *Memory of a Journey* (1951).
A powerful instance of materials that
have been substituted. Everything in this
interior has been transformed into stone:
the table, tablecloth, fruit bowl and fruit,
bottle and drinking glass, book, floor,
window, and landscape. The artist recalls
how, when he was a child, he and a
female friend would play in the abandoned
cemetery of a provincial Belgian town.
They would explore the crypts, pry open
the heavy iron trap doors, surrounded by
fraying columns and fallen leaves.

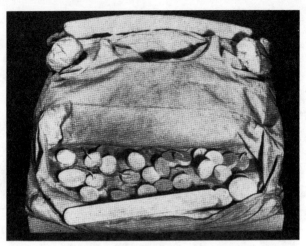

Claes Oldenburg, *Soft Typewriter 1* (1963).

In a now rare book, *Captain Cap*, the celebrated
humorist from the turn of the twentieth century,
Alphonse Allais, recounts how the famous captain
had crafted a violin out of wicker within which
he kept trained birds. When performing outdoors,
our busker would find a location between the poles
supporting telephone or power lines and, as he
was setting up, open a hatch in the back of his
violin. As he began to play (?)—I'm citing this from
memory because I can no longer locate my copy
of the book—a bird would exit at the sound of
each note and settle right on the corresponding line
of the staff.[24] Our performer was always careful, of
course, to find poles that supported five lines to
emulate the form of a music staff.

BED ON A MAIN SQUARE

Another facet of fantasy is the substitution of
locations. Someone sleeping in their bedroom and
their bed elicits no curiosity. But if, instead, they are
sleeping on a cathedral square with their bed, night
table, alarm clock, area rug, and pajamas, all in
the middle of passers-by as if this were completely
normal, people might well take notice.
A boat is usually encountered in the waters of a
sea or lake. But if we place it on a hilltop, it alters
that location as well as the balance between the
reasonable and unreasonable.
In his paintings Mr. de Chirico has presented us
with armoires and armchairs set in valleys and bed-
rooms containing an entire sea.[25] But we'd consider
a rowing machine placed in a bedroom for training
purposes perfectly natural.

An old Buster Keaton film highlights variations in
location. Cast in the role of projectionist, Buster
is tasked with remaining in his control booth for
the duration of the film. The problem is that he gets
caught up in the screen world and, alongside the
other actors, ends up participating in the action.
The comic effect results from the fact that the
setting regularly shifts and, as a result, Buster keeps
getting stuck in unpredictable jams.[26] Who can
forget the famous scene in *Hellzapoppin'* in which
"an Indian chief on horseback rides into the midst
of an elegant reception at a luxury villa?"[27] Again, a
change in location driven by a shift in the setting
of a film. Likewise, altered locations are frequent in
H. G. Wells's *Time Machine*. A scientist has invented
a machine that instead of permitting travel in space,
allows for travel in time. As a result, travelers are
free to experience prehistory or the future, as they
see fit.

One used to be able to find postcards in Milanese stationery stores that showed the city located seaside, with the Piazza del Duomo awash in seawater. The same principle of turning situations on their heads could be used to transform Venice into a city of streets clogged with automobiles.

The estrangement achieved by these exercises in fantasy is the result of relocating a familiar object in an unfamiliar place, much like a pigeon appearing the hat of an illusionist.

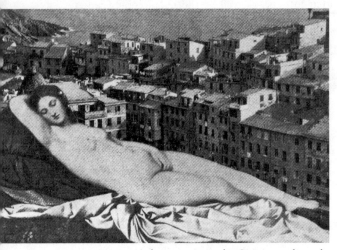

A famous painting by Giorgione relocated.

If Milan was on the sea. Humorous
postcard (1930s).

Many of Marcel Duchamp's works are based upon
shifts in place and function. When he exhibits a
bottle rack or a shovel or a bicycle tire in an art
gallery, he places it in a place that it is not its own,
an altered setting. The result is that the object takes
on a different function and an altered meaning.

Photo: Mario de Blasi.

A SHEET-MUSIC LAMPSHADE

Yet another facet of fantasy is the substitution of
functions. An object with a precise function is
selected and then employed for another function.
A drinking glass used as a vase for flowers, a bottle
used as a lampshade, a demijohn bottle with a little
light inside used as an accent lamp, a carriage lamp
used as a wall sconce, the scale model of a toilet
used as an ashtray, a large Mexican sombrero used
as a wall decoration, an antique crib used as a
magazine rack, an old iron safe used as a bar, a bar
used as a field of battle, a bottle used as a bomb.
Anyone can find additional examples that have
bubbled up out of the effervescence of popular
culture. In one of his films, Charlie Chaplin uses a
child's shoe as a coin purse and who can forget the
famous shoes "eaten" by Chaplin as if a tasty dish?[28]
Under the rubric of changes in function we can
also place farms or old mills (and similar buildings)
that have been repurposed as vacation homes.
In the United States I have seen an old barn transformed into the abode of a famous architect with
the old stalls left intact and horse blankets used
to cover sofas. Such adaptations are ubiquitous
in popular architecture magazines and sometimes
justified on economic grounds (though rarely so).

Truth or fantasy?

A strongbox is opened, exposing a backlit bar with
a thousand bottles of Bernardoni whiskey, Buganza
vodka, and other premium liquors. We drink. Hurrah!
We open an eighteenth-century Venetian cabinet and
a television lights up automatically. An ice cube is
extracted from a spherical ice bucket with a pair of
chicken-foot tongs. Let's assume that the tongs are
(or appear to be) made of gold. A golden light cascades
down through a music paper lampshade supported on
a long black flute (the candle-shaped light source
remains obscured). With a pig-shaped corkscrew we
uncork a bottle of Gazzoni Barolo while depositing
the ashes of a cigarette in a golden ceramic ashtray in
the shape of woman's hand. A trunk-like vase holds a
large bouquet of artificial flowers behind which looms
a trompe l'oeil painting of flowers with shredded
letters. There's legible writing on one of the shreds.
The hostess, in part painted and in part present,
smiles with utter spontaneity. The daughter of Madame
Wpz drops a vinyl onto a turntable hidden in another
eighteenth-century Venetian cabinet: it's a record by
[the impersonator] Alighiero Noschese who sounds like
a legion of people (it's really just him). We see that
it's 2 o'clock (a.m. or p.m.?) in a frying-pan-shaped
clock. Near the clock, there's a white ceramic pressing
iron ornamented with blue florets and dotted with
golden pinecones. A gentleman with dyed hair puffs
on a pipe shaped like the head of a black bull.
He's regaling an elderly woman (rejuvenated thanks to
cosmetic interventions) with tales about his seaside
villa shaped like a sailboat, complete with bookshelves
made of maritime ladders, a clock encased in a rudder,
wall sconces made out of boating lights, a trap door
entrance to the living room, a French-drain system in
the basement, and so many other genial features. The
lady isn't quite sure how to respond. But her daughter
(a former nun) volunteers that, at their house, they have
a chandelier made out of a steelyard scale and that
her architect husband owns a wide-brimmed Mexican
hat that he never wears, so he keeps it appended to
the dining room wall alongside a rifle-shaped key ring.
It's no longer fashionable to use carriage lights as
sconces or carriage wheels sawn in half as entry gates
for rural villas.

84

A child enters the room with a cobbler's hammer in his hand. He entertains himself by administering hammer blows to everyone. Everyone laughs politely. Madame Pzzb bustles about the living room serving purgative chocolates to the guests out of a fake violin case. There are few takers, so the dismayed Madame Pzzb sets the case down atop a fishtail-shaped piano alongside an image of the hostess as a child dressed as a sailor with the feathered hat of an army sharp-shooter.[29] The photo is nested inside a picture frame in the form of an oversized pocket watch. We light candles that look like Chinese statuettes and slot them into crystal-like plexiglass candleholders. Tux the cat, sleeping until this moment alongside a large ceramic dog, gets up and leaves. The child chases him in his bunny slippers but collides with a shoe-shaped um-brella stand. A pagoda umbrella comes tumbling down and breaks into a thousand pieces. A telephone shaped like a cushion rings; it's a wrong number. Sorry! says the voice at the other end. The evening is nearing its end. We say goodbye and thank the hosts who express dismay at our determination to leave.

Each guest grabs his or her coat off a deer-antler coatrack. A (hired) waiter opens a flush wall-mounted door, indistinguishable from the surrounding walls and there we are: in the middle of Broadway. We flag a taxicab and ask the driver to take us to SSkml. Sure thing, sssir! says the driver as he heads off in the direction of Mllrnh.

Another facet of fantasy is the modification of pace.
We refer to an accelerated version of a movement
ordinarily performed slowly as "movement Ridolini
style."[30] It was none other than this silent film actor
who perfected the use of the movie camera as an
expressive visual medium. Even today, aside from
zooming and other elementary effects, the full visual
potential of film remains underutilized. An event is
initially translated into words according to literary
norms and, only then, transposed into film. So many
films based on novels! Only scientific research
occasionally demonstrates how a proper use of a
movie camera can allow us to experience phenomena
that words can explain only with great difficulty.
So, the technical possibilities of film remain ripe for

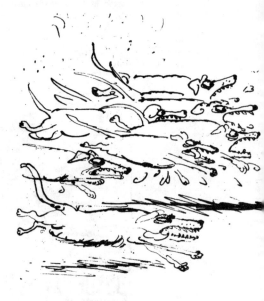

exploration. Every now and then, an author embraces them as a language. Think of Alain Robbe-Grillet's visual descriptions of settings, of films shot at one thousand or three thousand frames per second, or, on the contrary, of films shot at one frame per every two or ten minutes. Only the cinema allows us to see these fluctuations in temporality and, along with them, alterations in the motion of a phenomenon, not to mention gaining access to realities that can't be grasped by other means.

In 1964, there existed a laboratory devoted to experimentation with the language of cinema in Monte Olimpino, near Como.[31] It was in that same year that, with Marcello Piccardo and some friends, we shot a three-minute 16 mm film on the dilation of time. The film in question was carried out with a specialized piece of equipment called a "time microscope," borrowed from the science labs at the University of Milan. Normally used to drastically

Cartoon: Ronald Searle.

slow down movements that the human eye cannot perceive, the device allows you to see the explosion of a light bulb struck by a bullet or the splash of drops of milk landing in a saucer.[32] Many will have experienced these "real time" special effects on television which require filming at around 1500 frames per second (instead of the standard rate of twenty-four frames per second). When one projects the resulting image sequences at normal speeds the result is motion slowed in proportion to the original frame rate.

The film we created in 1964 was entitled *Tempo nel tempo* (Time within Time) and was shot at a rate of 3000 frames per second, which posed special challenges when it came to lighting the nine-square-meter stage on which an acrobat was to perform a backflip.[33] The action was chosen because it established a real time reference: you can't perform a backflip in more than a second. So, the difference between the backflip with which the film opens and the second version in which it takes three minutes for the acrobat to land is all the more palpable to the viewer. Slowed down to this extreme degree, his movement is barely perceptible, and you can readily observe all the micro-adjustments required to perform the backflip in a second. As will come as no surprise to anyone in the know, three minutes of projection time is a long time.

Changes in pace also occur when Superman flies, instead of when he runs. Or when, in a fable, a race takes place between a snail and a turtle. Or when one imagines what might happen if firemen moved at the speed of bureaucrats or bureaucrats moved at the speed of firemen.

Bruno Munari and Marcello Piccardo, some frame sequences from *Tempo nel tempo*, shot at 3,000 frames per second, Studio di Monte Olimpino (1964).

A performer from the
White Horse Circus, a work
by the Bread and Puppet
Theater, directed by Peter
Schumann. The immediate
impact of a change in scale.
Photo: Antonio Sferlazzo.

Changes in scale are another facet of fantasy.
Pop art exploded in the 1960s. People marveled
at seeing the same sorts of oversized objects they
had encountered in international trade fairs exhibited at the world's most famous art galleries. In
these mass audience marketplaces for new industrial
products, PR agents applied the formula of massive
upscaling to attract the attention of the public.
We can all recall seeing enormous tubes of toothpaste or gigantic cans of motor oil and their like
hovering in the skies above such fairs. These gas-
filled balloons made of rubber were always cabled
to the ground. What is called Pop art has always
proliferated at such events. Which is to say that
these objects were unsurprising to the mass audience, but not to art critics when they encountered
them in an altered location. What was once a trade
fair featuring unsigned objects has become an art
biennial of expensive signed artworks.

Installations at trade fairs and world's fairs
have always sought to astound the public
with changes in scale. This example from
1960 shows a tire with a diameter of thirty
meters. Compare the tire to the human
figures below.

92

A 130-meter-tall water jet which varies
in shape with the wind created in the
early twentieth century by Emile Merle
d'Aubigné on Lake Geneva. Today we'd
refer to it as a water sculpture.

There are small rocks that resemble
mountains. All you have to do
is look at them that way and they
change dimension.

Evening Shadow, bronze statue from
the Hellenistic period.

Bruno Munari, *Peace Trumpet* (1950).
A military trumpet flattened out into
two dimensions.

Changes in scale are frequent in science fiction films
in the pursuit of startling and impressive effects.
The first example that comes to mind is King Kong,
the gigantic gorilla, who climbs atop the tallest
skyscraper in New York with a young woman in his
paw—beautiful, to emphasize the contrast—where
he has to fight off a squadron of fighter jets that are
swarming about, threatening to kill him.
It's interesting to know how these effects were staged.
Naturally, King Kong was a large, hinged model
built on a steel skeleton to which rubber muscles had
been attached so that they move like actual animal
muscles. Forty bear skins were required to cover his
body; six human operators were needed to animate
his motions from within. The giant gorilla's voice was
created by recording the roar of a lion, reducing the
pitch by an octave, and playing it backwards.

A scene from *King Kong* (1933).

There were many successors to this 1933 film that similarly exploited alterations in scale. One of these was *Them!* (1954) in which giant insects invade our planet but are eventually exterminated with flamethrowers. A film entitled *Tarantula* followed one year later with a ghastly spider starring as a gigantic monster.[34]

All these shifts in scale present their audiences with a fait accompli: the monster has already assumed enormous, overwhelming proportions. Another film, based on a novel by Richard Matheson and released in 1956, is built instead around gradual, almost imperceptible changes in scale. Sunbathing on the deck of his boat, a man is suddenly enshrouded in a strange fog. He initially ignores the phenomenon. But after a couple of days he comes to realize that his clothes are now too large. He weighs himself and realizes that, despite being in good health, he has lost weight. A visit to the doctor produces no explanation. As he continues to diminish in size, he is studied by other doctors and placed under observation in a special clinic but with no results. His wife's dimensions remain normal; she tries to take care of him and to provide emotional support, to no avail. The man continues shrinking. He finds it increasingly difficult to make use of even the simplest tools, only to eventually shrink to microscopic scale and to disappear into a sparkling starlit night sky.[35]

Another recent film plays out shifts in scale in the opposite direction. A team of scientists and their submarine-like ship are miniaturized so that they can be injected into a human body to seek out and neutralize a cancerous growth.[36]

Back in the era when ships took a long time to cross oceans, sailors were wont to build miniatures of the ships they were sailing on (or of other ships) inside empty bottles. The models were built outside the bottle with the trees and sails folded. The vessel was then slid into the bottle while keeping threads (tied to the miniature trees) outside. The model was anchored in the proper location in a layer of stucco and then, pulling on the threads, the trees were stood up and the sails unfurled: just like opening an umbrella. Then the threads were cut. Today oceans are crossed in only a few hours and stewardesses barely have the time to empty out bottles, which is why one doesn't encounter jumbo jets in Coca-Cola bottles.

A sailing ship in a bottle nearing the shore.

A scene from the film *Them!* (1954).

For millennia, small dwarf trees known as *bonsai* have been cultivated in the Far East, always with the aim of leaving intact all of the object's core characteristics despite the shift in scale. When photographed without showing the vase in which they are growing, these dwarf trees look like full-sized trees. Just like other trees, they are actual trees that live outdoors and can lead protracted lives. I saw a beautiful, thriving nine-hundred-year-old bonsai in Kyoto at the home of a grower. Another facet of Asian culture related to shifts in scale is the perception that certain stones or rocks are mountain-like or, to be more precise, like miniatures of massive mountains. When photographed in the right light and blown up, they readily produce the desired effect on a viewer who is unable to perceive the change in scale.

An exceptional 70-centimeter-tall bonsai.
Bonsai are dwarf trees that have been long
(maybe forever) grown in China and Japan.
A tree adapts to the ground in which
it grows: in northern climes, Oleanders
are bushes; in southern climes, they are
tall trees. Plants adapt themselves to the
environment and create new species. From
bonsai seed are born other bonsai trees.
Bonsai lovers particularly prize those trees
that were born and grown in difficult
settings: in the cleft in a rock, in the
walls of a home perched on a cliff, in the

amazing places to which seeds are carried by the wind. They remove them from there without ruining their roots and place them in vases or ceramic trays where they can be attended to with great care. I have seen 900-year-old bonsai in Japan. You can verify the health of the plant by the color of its leaves.

They are trees like other trees. They grow outdoors, not inside homes. In Italy, when one-year-old plants arrive from abroad at the local nursery, one can go and pick out those that the nursery personnel consider the ugliest (because they are bent). Ignorant people always want straight, symmetrical plants. What they don't realize is that crooked ones are more interesting.

Artists who don't have a lot of ideas use shifts in scale to continue to produce in the same style. Let's say an artist becomes famous for painting a hammer white. In his next exhibition he will paint a violin white, then a motorcycle, a public monument, a house, or a triumphal arch. To further astonish the public, he will go on to paint a forest, a hill, a (small) island…. No doubt, there will be a limit. But he becomes known as "the one who paints stuff white."

And before wrapping up this topic, let's not forget the change in proportions in Pinocchio's nose when he tells a lie.

Alessandro Mendini, *Haybale Chair*,
(1974), three meters tall.

Cartoon: Ronald Searle.

There was an Old Man of Coblenz,
The length of whose legs was immense;
He went with one prance
From Turkey to France,
That surprising Old Man of Coblenz.
—Edward Lear, *A Book of Nonsense.*

There was an Old Man, on whose nose,
Most birds of the air could repose;
But they all flew away
At the closing of day,
Which relieved that Old Man and his nose.
—Edward Lear, *A Book of Nonsense.*

Two nonsense poems by Edward Lear.

Igor Stravinsky, *The Soldier's Tale*, Teatro de Buratto, Milan. Photo: Renato Biffi.

The evil beast, a popular Spanish print.

A TERRIFYING MONSTER

Another facet of fantasy involves the fusion of varied components within a single body. The components can originate from animals: different animals such that, deftly composed, a monster is born. Monsters are infinitely varied: Paolo Uccello's in his painting *Saint George and the Dragon* has what appears to be a canine head (with strange teeth), a stocky and lean body with the rib cage and spinal column fully visible, only two very muscular legs with three-toed paws and powerful talons, a pair of wings that may perhaps belong to a bat but are decorated with large disks, and a long and curly ribbed tail. Hieronymus Bosch is rightly considered the master of such fantasies which abound in his works.

In summary, a great many artists, in particular painters, have embraced this typology on various occasions and to various ends.

There are alternative ways of combining animal parts with non-animal components. Think of Dali's female figures with chests of drawers nested in their bodies or of Frankenstein, a semiartificial monster, whose body includes a metal faucet implanted in his neck.

The Fly, a 1957 sci-fi film, tells the story of a scientist who, thanks to a flawed experiment with a molecular transporter, ends up with the head of a common house fly that was present by accident in the laboratory. The insect interloper, now endowed with a human head, can be heard crying out: "Help!", as it is about to be devoured by a spider.[37]

In 1959, the famous Lon Chaney appeared on the silver screen transformed into a human crocodile.[38] Sirens and centaurs were the first expressions of this mode of fantasy. We encounter human figures with the head of a bird or a bull in ancient Egyptian art.

When it comes to household objects, it suffices to think of how common claw-foot furniture is, and tables and other furniture with animal legs of various kinds.

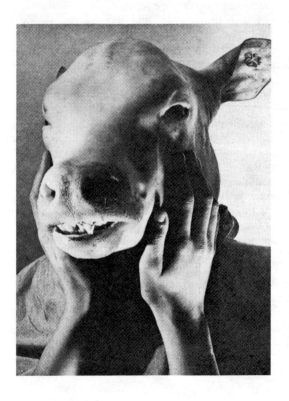

Erwin Blumenfeld, *Self-portrait with a Mask or Minotaur* (1936).

The sun god Ra Horakhty, ca. 9th century BCE).

Monsters drawn by J. J. Grandville.

René Magritte, *The Collective Invention* (1934). Here's an instance of the fusion of two different elements—a human body and a fish body—but with the substitutions reversed. Is the result a failed siren?

Humanized animals or, rather,
men and women with animal heads.
Drawing: J. J. Grandville.

A FORMIDABLE WEIGHTLIFTER

Another facet of fantasy involves altering the weight of an object.

We are at an equestrian circus. The lights come on and at the center of the ring appears the most famous weightlifter in the world. He is dressed in a black leotard and black wrestling boots. He stands close to the weight he is about to lift. The weight is resting on a red carpet; it's an iron bar with a watermelon-sized iron sphere at each end.

The acrobat smiles at the audience and waves before squatting to grasp the barbell. A long drum roll sounds and the weightlifter swiftly hoists the weight to the height of his chest on which it now rests. In the silence that follows he tries to complete the lift, turns beet red, his muscles shudder, the weight rises. It's almost at the height of his nose. Slowly it moves upward. Now its above his head! He is completely still for a moment, his arms outstretched, his eyes cast upward. The audience can feel his effort. But what is happening? The feet of the acrobat are no longer in contact with the ground. They take off slowly. The entire acrobat with barbell upraised ascends slowly and gradually disappears into the darkness of the circus dome.

René Magritte, *The Castle of the Pyrenees*
(1959). An instance of a change in weight:
a boulder hovers motionlessly in the air
while the sea moves beneath it.

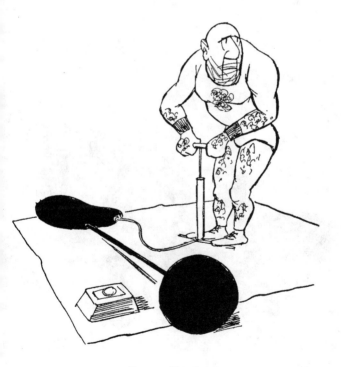

Cartoon: Chaval.

J. J. Grandville, *An Odd Sculptor* (ca. 1830).

In the preceding chapters I have tried to bring some elementary examples of the combined use of fantasy, invention, and creativity into focus. There may be other or better examples. My aim has been to see whether it's possible to understand (and, therefore, to explain) how these human abilities function.
If others reflect on this and wish to revise my thoughts, they are doing me a big favor. Thanks in advance! You are helping me and others to come to a better understanding of these matters.

Another, more complex, instance of the workings of fantasy, invention, and creativity involves connections between connections.
We have seen some basic instances involving the alteration or substitution of a real attribute with a fictitious one. Cases in point: a blue cat, a fast turtle, a heavy butterfly, a sofa at the bottom of a swimming pool, and so on. If we combine these cases of novel combinations, we end up with a more complex result. An example: a blue cat (simple change in color) so light it must be tied down to keep from floating off (change in weight), who is twenty meters tall (change in scale), and is striding through a blazing fire (change in location), etc. Complex creations result that provoke, in turn, amusing effects.
And these aren't all the combinations of attributes available to me. I haven't even introduced variations and alterations of sensory receptors. So now our famous ultralight, twenty-meter-tall, fire-walking blue cat barks, appears deep frozen, and its body emits the sweetish scent of patchouli. Perhaps this qualifies our cat as the star of an upcoming sci-fi film?
Other components of a cultural character allow for further complexity. For example, as you can see in

Man Ray's retouched photograph *Ingres's Violin*, the image isn't just inspired by the formal parallelism between a violin and the back of a woman with two f-holes painted in, but rather by the fact that Ingres himself played the violin.

All of these instances of fantasy at work don't amount to a recipe for transforming oneself into a brilliantly creative inventor. Oil paints don't make paintings; or as Duchamp nicely put it: "it isn't the *colla* [glue] that makes a collage."[39]

On the contrary, the analysis of simple and complex case studies helps us to comprehend fantasy's logic, instruments, and modus operandi, though completion requires refinement and culture. All of these processes have rules that, even if the rules are invented, they remain teachable. Otherwise, all this would be a purely subjective exercise, self-referential in nature, useful perhaps only for purposes of experimentation or research.

It isn't by stealing Rafael's paintbrush that one becomes a great painter.

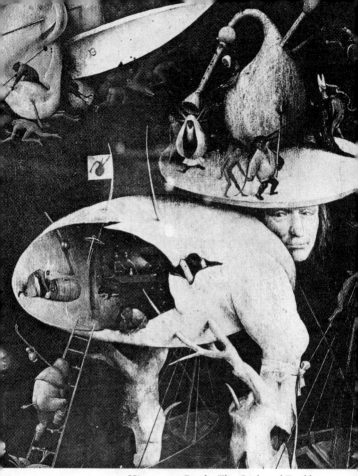

Hieronymus Bosch, *The Garden of Earthly Delights* (detail).

Everything that a child memorizes will remain present in memory and shape the child's personality. It is up to us adults to convey to children all those forms of knowledge that will help them to achieve understanding and to engage creatively with other people.

Creativity, which is the purposeful use of fantasy and invention, continuously forms and transforms. It requires a quick and flexible intelligence, a mind that is free of all sorts of preconceptions, ready to rise to every new challenge, and willing to alter its opinions when a better one comes along.

Creative individuals are thus in continuous evolution and their creative powers are the result of a continuous updating and expansion of their knowledge base in all domains.

An uncreative individual is an imperfect individual. His mind finds it difficult to tackle problems that present themselves without the help of a creative person.

A creative person is both a recipient of and a contributor to the culture of a community, flourishing alongside it. An uncreative person is usually an individualist who stubbornly pits their beliefs against those of others like them.

It is better to tackle societal rather than individual problems. Societal problems concern the collectivity, an aggregate that has always existed and that will continue to exist so long as there are individuals. The cultural growth of the collectivity depends upon us as individuals, upon what we contribute to it. We are the collectivity.

Our future society is already present among us in the form of children. Our ability to shape a more or less free and creative future society depends upon how children grow and develop. To this end, we must free children from all useless restrictions and help them to flourish. The goal is to nurture the growth every personality such that it can contribute to collective growth.

Infants shouldn't be buried in obligations, constrained by schemes that aren't their own, pushed to replicate existing models. One of the most common ways to extinguish the slightest spark of creativity in children of this age is, for example, to assign a drawing on a fixed theme to be executed with the same tools, be they markers or watercolors or tempera paints. Sometimes it seems as if only painting and sculpture are available to express oneself in the visual arts in Italian and other nursery and elementary schools. Accordingly, boys and girls are handed paintbrushes or temperas or, in the case of three-dimensional work, clay or other plastic materials. Technical information is rarely provided, leaving children to their own devices. Many instructors and nursery school teachers claim, "We give children complete freedom to do as they choose, we provide them with paints and clay so that they may express themselves freely." But if the horizons of these same children are not expanded by being exposed to creative play, they will not succeed in building connections between things they know or will do so in a very limited manner, with the result that their faculty of fantasy will remain underdeveloped. The vast majority of children throughout the world paint the same things. They paint what they see, that which they know: a field, a house, mountains, a tree, and the sun. The form of the house or tree may vary, but the subject matter remains more or less the same. And if they aren't encouraged to develop, they will paint the same things in the same way as adult hobbyists.

So, creativity needs to be nourished. But how? By inventing games from which children can keep learning new things, acquire new skills, and come to understand the rules of visual language. Every drawing contains a message. But if this message isn't developed in accord with the rules of visual language, that message will not be received. No visual communication will have been established, which is to say, no communication.

To learn how to explain to children what a rule is and how rules function, ask a child to explain one of the many rules they have invented and employed in their games. You might, for instance, ask them the name of a game played on a piece of pavement on which you have drawn a bell-shaped form in chalk, dividing it up into an uneven number of sections, and then tossing a pebble inside the drawing. A child will respond right away and explain the rules: you toss the pebble, you jump inside the drawing without touching the chalk lines…. These are the rules of hopscotch (or as it sometimes known, *gioco del mondo*). Now let's find out what the rules are for the growth of a plant. Let's see how a tree grows.[40]

> What is most needed is not more aesthetics or more esoteric manuals of art education but a convincing case made for visual thinking quite in general. Once we understand in theory, we might try to heal in practice the unwholesome split which cripples the training of reasoning power.
> —Rudolph Arnheim, *Visual Thinking*

As a game, one can also furnish children with sheets of paper of highly varied size and format: 10-by-140-centimeter rectangles cut from bundles of wrapping paper 1.4 meters in width.

Square, triangular, oval, irregular, rhomboid, and odd-shaped sheets created by cutting or ripping paper. Sheets that are large or even gigantic, small or even tiny. The sheets should be cut on the fly, in front of the children. No need for explanations. All that is required is an invitation extended to each child to select the sheet he or she prefers for drawing or painting on with whatever method the sheet suggests to them. As experiments carried out in Italy and other countries suggest, this exercise leads to the creation of much more varied images than usual. Many teachers have been stunned by the result because, seeing the enthusiasm of their peers, some children who have never drawn before are suddenly inspired to.

Drawings by six- and seven-year-old
children. The subject of each artwork was
inspired by the sheet of paper that the
child freely selected from among sheets
of highly variable size and format.
Photo: Bruno Nencioni.

It makes good sense that a narrow and long piece
of paper, viewed horizontally, would bring to mind
things that share that same shape: a snake, an auto
race, a train, a tree-lined boulevard, a submarine in
the ocean.... If instead viewed vertically, the same
sheet of paper suggests other images to a child: a
missile, a tower, a skyscraper.... What can be said
with certainty is that, when observing a child who
is contemplating what he or she will draw on a
given sheet of paper, we can perceive the intimations
of creativity or fantasy by studying the child's facial
expressions.

Four-, five-, and six-year-old children have drawn
things that they never would have on the standard
paper formats handed out in school settings.

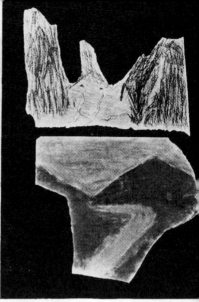

Teachers who wish to tackle these questions—let's
hope there will always be more of them!—must
offer children an endlessly novel array of ancient
and modern techniques to choose from in the form
of play: from tempera to watercolors, prints, etchings,
splashed-on colors, painting on water-soaked paper,
collages made with tissue paper, cardboard, cutout
newspaper images, colors made with cornstarch,
glues, sponges, stamps, monotypes, floating colors,
projections of materials, mosaics of paper, colored
powder, and material assemblages.

In the domain of three-dimensional constructions,
a good starting point is the transformation of a
two-dimensional sheet into a three-dimensional
object. In Japan children are taught how to make
origami: objects or figures of animals or flower
created by repeatedly folding a sheet of paper.
This is an exercise that teaches children precision.

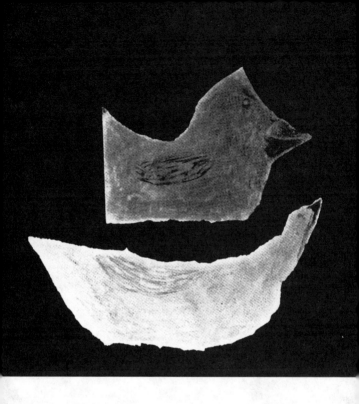

Constructions can be made with iron wires, cardboard tubes, plastic objects, boxes, egg cartons:
the thousands of things that enter our homes as
packaging and that we throw away. Many teachers
are aware of these methods, but it is essential that
they be presented to children one at a time, with
explanations of their material and technical characteristics, the ways they can be used, how they can
be stuck together, to teach the rules, explain the
challenges, and then let children do as they see fit.
Never impose a theme.
If unfamiliar with these methods, you can call up
a friend who is a decorator or a window display
designer to explain to both children and adults these
opportunities for visual and design education.

A free drawing by a young girl from
Camaiore. Free drawing is a method
for keeping one's thought process flexible
and staying away from static solutions.
As the child draws, the meaning continuously shifts.

DIRECT PROJECTIONS

Among the newest techniques of interest to children is the direct projection of materials.[41] All you need is an inexpensive slide projector and some slides. It's a technique that is especially engaging because it moves at the speed of thought. Whereas it takes a long time to finish up a drawing executed with colored pencils and markers, a large and luminous projection of the child's work can be created almost instantly. If the result isn't satisfactory, all you have to do is open up the slide, alter the composition, and verify the outcome.[42] The child knows that if he sandwiches a little feather into his slide, he'll see a gigantic tree in the projection! Onion skins produce quirky effects. A piece of gauze, when it is project- ed, looks like a fishing net. Every material serves as a stimulus to fantasy and gives rise to new images. The initial results are mostly random. Children need

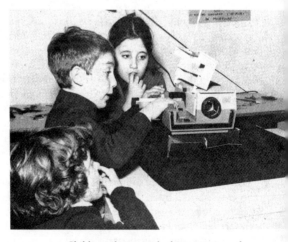

Children playing with the projection of slides that they have crafted out of colored transparent materials.

to be invited to select any old material and place it within the slide without any concern for what will result. Then the slide is projected on a white wall, on the ceiling, or a screen (if one is available). This has the advantage of allowing everyone to participate, even those children who are afraid to make mistakes when they draw. When you call it a game, inferiority complexes vanish. Then it's time to look at the slides together in the semidarkness of the room where they can be projected on the largest possible scale. Everyone is invited to say what comes to mind when viewing the images. The intentional use of the effects obtained by these techniques commences after the exercise has been concluded.

How to implement this experiment.

This case study may be of value for all sorts of techniques (with the requisite adjustments, naturally). One day, a teacher enters the classroom with a slide projector in hand. She opens the box, unboxes the projector, lifts off the cover to show its internal workings (to whatever degree possible), and explains how it functions. She puts the cover back on and the other components back together, places the projector on a table, plugs it in, and a stream of light is projected on the white wall. If the projector isn't too bulky, if it's a small projector, the teacher can pick it up and move the light beam around the ceiling and walls, as if it were a searchlight. Then she opens another box containing a slide tray and extracts a slide frame from the tray: the sort of slide frame that can be splayed open like a book, with glass panels attached on two sides. She pulls a photographic slide out of her pocket (she brought a few of landscapes and the like) and places it into the frame which she snaps closed with her fingers, showing the children precisely how this is done. She places the slide in the

130

slide projector and begins projecting. She explains how you focus the image. She shows how to change slides. One or many images can be projected depending on the time available. She has a dialogue with the children, encouraging the asking of questions, providing technical answers.

The next day the teacher will have a camera with her, either hers or that of a parent, one that takes fixed-focus pictures in the same format as that of the projector. Children are invited to photograph anything, whether an animal, a landscape, or something else that appeals to them. It's best if every child takes at least one color photograph.

On another day, the children's color photographs are projected so that every child can see what the others have chosen to photograph, how the photos were shot or came out, and to discuss technical matters. In order to thwart competitive or imitative urges, there will be no value judgments pronounced. Compositions will be analyzed, backgrounds studied, frontal and back-lighting examined. Everyone will have done their best and will be helped to do even better.

The following day the slide projector will still be there but there won't be any slides. The question becomes: What can you do with a projector without slides? The projector is turned on and the light beam interrupted with a variety of hand gestures that produce interesting shadows. A transparent object, a drinking glass, or a printed glass ashtray can be thrust into the light beam as well, rotating each object so as to produce a variety of shadows bearing traces of light.

A child is sent to the janitor to borrow a feather duster. The duster arrives and the teacher pulls out a single feather and embeds it in a slide frame. She places the slide frame in the projector and everyone can now see the makeup of a feather. It looks as if

The lattice-like vein structure of a leaf.

it were a tree or something else. A snippet of colored paper is slotted into another slide frame; when projected, its color isn't visible. Other tests follow and the class discovers that all transparent things project their colors, while all opaque things project only a black shadow.

After a discussion, everyone agrees to come back the next day with samples of materials to see what happens when one projects them.

A little inventory is drawn up: onion and garlic

An onion skin.

peels, flower petals, cotton wool, gauze, wax, wool
and cotton threads, colored transparent vellum, old
film stock, black-and-white or failed photographs....
The next day, the materials brought in by the
children are collected and studied. Small samples are
more than adequate. The teacher, of course, will also
have brought something in—some transparent vellum
paper of the sort found at a stationer, a dried-out
veined leaf, a veil, a piece of wax paper, etc. All
the materials are tested to establish what works or

Every material reveals its structure.

doesn't work. The teacher runs the tests, placing
each sample in a slide frame and projecting it to see
the results. A list of materials that still need to
be gathered is eventually worked up as a function
of the materials already assembled.

A day later, fun is had by composing and projecting
everything that has been brought into school. The
materials can be used separately or combined. But
it's best not to try to squeeze too much material into
a single slide because a confusing image will result;
when slides become too thick it also becomes difficult to slot them into the projector and they tend to
lock up the slide tray. Children are entirely free to
create as they see fit so long as they don't damage
the machinery which belongs to everyone. Every
child will experiment, make slides, toss out the ones
he or she doesn't like, rework them until the result
is satisfying. The teacher will collect all the successful slides, including at least one from every child,

134

and organize a final comprehensive slide show. The projection of each slide will be accompanied by an explanation from its creator of how it was made and what it shows that is distinctive, new, or strange. Each child will, thus, give voice to the image he or she has composed as it is projected.

At the end of the session, the overall question of what can be done with these images, what they can be used for, will be raised. How so? We will soon see.

On another day, the teacher proposes experiments with the projection of foams and colored inks. A drop of colored ink is dripped onto soap, a colored foam is formed by stirring with a finger, the foam is loaded into the slide and is thus projected. Every child gets to choose a color or India ink color. (In actuality, only the three primary colors are essential: cold blue, lemon yellow, and magenta red; from these all the other colors can be mixed.) A blob

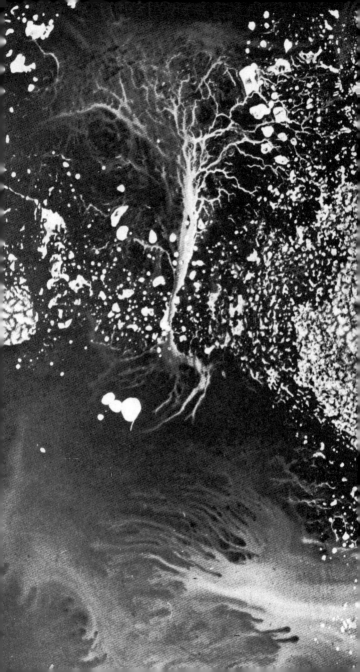

of foam is formed, it's placed in the slide, and gets projected. These effects can also be greatly blown up because their natural structure is beautiful on any scale. While a drawing on a slide executed with a marker doesn't project well—sheets of paper are present for just this purpose—natural forms, whether cut or torn, retain their structural characteristics, like the lattice-like vein structure of a leaf, a paper-thin slice of expanded polyester, a shred of wax paper, or a net.

> On the preceding page you can see the results of the large-scale projection of a slide prepared with colored inks. The slide was prepared by Mario de Biasi who, in addition to being a famous photographer, is also known for his experiments with new ways of creating images that employ simple procedures.

On another occasion, all the expressive means can be mixed together: colored foams with gauzes or powders or veils or transparent vellum or wax. A piece of a candle can be employed to trace a sign on a slide (perhaps a letter of the alphabet?). A drop of color is added and, once again, it's time to project. By the end of this process, there will be a significant quantity of slides for the teacher to select and collect.

On yet another occasion, the teacher poses a question: we've made so many slides—what can we do with them? How might we make even them useful? We begin by ordering the slides according to image sequences, grouping them by color or by material or by possible meaning. We explore whether a story can be developed in the form a little show to celebrate.... After various attempts, the decision is made to stage the show. But exactly how? There are slides that evoke the seabed or forests or geographic maps or landscapes viewed from above, as well as

other settings. We set out to plan the work. Will it be best to project slides on a screen from behind and to have the action unfold up front?
Rear projection is decided upon, and the projection surface will be tracing paper (like that used by architects and engineers).

Small plant seeds.

A work group is organized, a plan is hatched. The tracing paper backdrop will about one-and-a-half meters tall and two-and-a-half meters wide. It will be glued to an upper track of wood and kept taut by being affixed to a lower track as well. It will hang in midair, ten centimeters above the ground, attached to a horizontal wire that crosses the room. The projection is from behind but remains perfectly visible from in front, which is where the action will unfold. It's like standing in front of a bedsheet drying on a clothesline with the images changing on command. A few children have prepared the wire, others have located the wooden tracks, others have served as helpers. A true group effort: they write the text collaboratively and imagine the event as a happening built around improvisations staged in front of the projected images. All do a fine job.

Children showing their parents the slides
they have prepared for the slide show.
The children themselves serve as slide
operators.

The materials involved in this exercise are priceless
in the literal sense that they cost nothing: a feather,
a thread, a drop of liquid glue, an onion skin, a
pinch of cotton wool, a gram of wax, some small
flower seeds, the piece of a veil the size of a postage
stamp, some gauze, some snippets of transparent
colored vellum...

From this experience one can derive a set of principles that are valid also for other techniques of visual communication.

First, every tool that is used needs to be well understood so that it is used appropriately and knowledgeably.
Second, establish the techniques best suited to the tool in question.
Third, let every individual choose and decide what they wish to do with the knowledge they have acquired.
Fourth, analyze and discuss all results together—not to decide who is the most gifted but to understand the individual reasoning that went into each work.
Fifth, encourage and coordinate teamwork in the service of a spectacular end result.
Sixth, undo and redo everything so that it's constantly updated, and one doesn't mystify the finished work.

Knowledge of tools and techniques is fundamental. Just as proper verbal communication requires a correct understanding of words and the rules that govern their arrangement in discourse, so it is with visual communication. How could it be otherwise? To admit as much doesn't extinguish one's personality. It's absolutely mistaken to think that ignorance provides the maximum of freedom. On the contrary, knowledge endows individuals with mastery over the tool, enabling them to express themselves with clarity and coherence in the passage from medium to message. Gross failures in coherence are commonplace: thousands of works of visual art contain messages that remain little more than intentions on the part of the transmitter or author. They simply aren't transmitted to the receiver or audience for whom they are intended.
We have seen paintings weighed down with theory, social critique, religious meanings, or expressions of

personal anguish. All are messages that could have been more effectively conveyed in another medium such as literature or film. Instead, someone "born" as a painter tries to speak their piece on every conceivable subject matter relying upon painting to communicate what painting struggles to communicate. The very dynamism of Futurist paintings becomes static when one confines it within a picture frame, conveying a confusing message to a public that can't grasp its message. Movement, speed, and various temporal dimensions can't be expressed with static techniques; better to make use of kinetic media like film or kinetic art.[43]

Group discussion of individual works helps to clear up many questions for everyone. It confirms whether or not the message transmitted has been received. It sheds light on how a message has been received and the reasons for the specific mode of reception. Such explorations are useful to everyone: they expand understanding, refine individual's means of visual communication, and clarify the nature of choices.

Teamwork is thus the aggregate of all these values, the combination of highly varied personalities working together, each contributing their individual best, to the creation of an outcome that is purposeful, useful to the collectivity, and expands collective understanding in the process.

In this distinctive period of childhood, the destruction of the group's work is to be understood as a means to prevent the creation of models for future imitation, the "museification" of the work, the emergence of a star system of creators. It's not the object that needs to be preserved but rather the process, the method, the experimental framework that is always open for adaptation and application to newly formulated questions. The mind must remain ready, free, and flexible; the sole models to which it commits need to be in the service of culture and study. Creativity, fantasy, and invention need to be perpetually available and operate in perfect harmony. Preconceptions, rigid ideas, formulaic models, conventional styles are to be avoided. All are hindrances to the free exercise of creativity. Modes of inquiry and experimentation should never be finalized until one knows the precise outcome; only thereafter can the results in question be finalized. Innovative solutions to questions of visual communication—in the past we would have spoken instead of "art education"—necessarily arise from the effective usage of fantasy, invention, and creativity, operating within the framework of the proper working methodology. To be clear, there's no way to establish a firm boundary line between fantasy, invention, and creativity. The definitions formulated in the preceding chapters were merely efforts to see if it might be possible to articulate some operational distinctions in the hopes of facilitating the best possible conjoined use. It's safe to say that fantasy, invention, and creativity mostly work with the imagination simultaneously. There are probably no temporal asynchronies in our use of these capabilities. Creativity is thus to be understood as the purposive use of human capabilities in the most comprehensive manner possible. As such, what we sought to split apart and analyze in the first part of the book has been put back together again, yet cognizant of the fact that these faculties can be employed hereafter with a greater sense of clarity and efficacy.

Long exposure photograph of light paths traced with a flashlight.

TODAY AT SCHOOL ...

BEANS

<u>March 5</u>

Today we ate bean soup. The cook gave us some dry beans as a present.

EXPANDING KNOWLEDGE

Let's increase our knowledge by means of observation.
This is how the teachers at the Ponte Ronca Elementary School in Bologna taught their students about embryos and their role in the reproduction of plants.
From the pages of the school newsletter (issue 7, 1975–76).

We looked at the beans:

exterior:
 ←——— outer skin

Let's split the skinned bean down the middle.
On the inside there's a little yellow limb:
it's the <u>embryo</u>.

interior: embryo

Luana asks:

What is an
embryo?

To respond to her question we
performed an experiment:

We placed the beans in two glass vases.

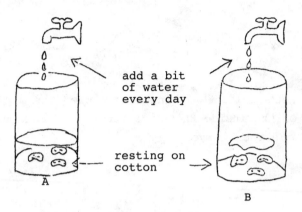

add a bit of water every day

resting on cotton

We removed the embryos from the beans in vase A. The beans in vase B have an embryo.

March 10
The beans in vase A remain the same.

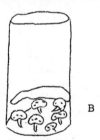

Five beans in vase B have sprouted.

March 15

The beans in vase A are all rotting.
We throw them away.

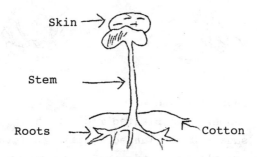

The beans in vase B now have yellow
roots growing downward and a green stem
growing upward.

March 16

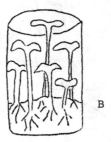

A little plant has grown out of each of
the six beans in vase B.

2nd experiment

In the meantime we planted some additional
seeds on the bed of cotton

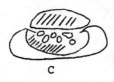

C

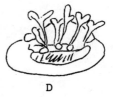

D

In saucers C and D.
In saucer C we planted rice (with no embryo).
In saucer D we planted lentils and grain.
Today, all the seeds in D germinated; none
of seeds in C.

We can therefore conclude:

An embryo is that
part of a seed from
which a new plant
germinates

THE WHOLE CLASS OF 1A

152

Bruno Munari, *Message In a Bottle* (ca. 1945). Often there is a postscript added to a message. What would a postscript look like in the case of a message in a bottle? It be written and then inserted into a smaller bottle attached to the main bottle with the main message by a cord. But where's the attachment point? At the waist: the waist featured on certain bottles of mint liqueur.[44]

A CREATIVE GAME

Stimulating childhood creativity in an elementary school in Milan. Around eighty children actively participated in playing a creative game. There's no need to explain to children what should be done: it's better to simply do it and the children will understand. At the same time, teachers and parents can help out with the exercise. They can provide answers to questions, help to maintain the children's focus for extended periods, explain rules that apply to understanding the external world in the form of a game, and clear up any doubts that arise from verbal accounts of what is transpiring. Will the children

understand? That's the best way to tell
whether the experiment is successful.
Experiments of this kind (and others
as well) have been carried out in
various kindergartens and elementary
schools abroad.

They rely upon a capacity that is always
active in children: curiosity. When a
child sees an adult do something, they
want to see it and then want to do it
themselves. This is the most direct route
to teach something to children without
lots of words, not to mention restrictions.
Children are always there, ready and
eager for something new to happen.

155

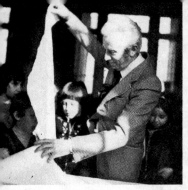

The facilitator takes hold of a large-format sheet of wrapping paper and begins by placing it on the gymnasium floor.
He then rips a second sheet lengthwise and places it at a V-angle with respect to the first.
Then he rips another pair of half-sheets lengthwise and attaches them to the first branch. He continues along these lines until he has built a big flat tree.
"Can someone give me a hand?" he asks. "Is there anyone who knows how to use Scotch tape?"
Some children begin attaching new branches of the big tree right away as it continues to grow until its smallest branches nearly fill the entire gymnasium.

Next the facilitator invites the children
to do something with the tree: to draw
anything that comes to mind in the
medium of their choice: markers, pastels,
paper cuttings, temperas, whatever they
wish. Each child is free to choose and
makes decisions on their own. Some need
a bit of time to make up their minds.
Some cut sheets of paper into leaflike
shapes, some draw squirrels or birds' nests.
Others draw insects, lizards, flowers, and
fruits: all sorts of things one finds in trees.
After a while the room calms down.
Some are still completing their drawings;
others are wandering around on top of
the big flat tree.

At this juncture, the facilitator proposes that the tree be detached from the ground and raised up into the air. Everyone altogether now! The children rush to seize the tree; they lift it off the ground and make it fly. The tree breaks up into a thousand pieces. The children are overjoyed. The event is transformed into a big party with paper flying everywhere. The game concludes, thus, with all the players happy. The tree is no more. But what remains is not a model to be copied, but rather a method that allows for the construction of future trees, each one unlike the other, built according to exactly the same core principle regarding the growth of trees illustrated by the game: namely, that, as the facilitator demonstrated, each subsequent branch is smaller than the one that precedes it.[45]

ROSES IN THE SALAD[46]

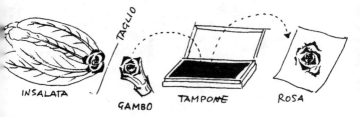

INSALATA   TAGLIO   GAMBO   TAMPONE   ROSA

Prints made by slicing plants and using them as stamps that can be inked with stamp pads of various colors.

This mode of image creation is ideal for children who refuse to draw because they were thoughtlessly scolded by parents inattentive to such matters, allowing them to participate in a game without any fear of making mistakes.

The true mistake is, of course, that made by the parents who believe that drawings should faithfully reproduce reality. On the contrary, drawing, particularly for children, is a mode of expression of universal (i.e., not merely visual) sensations, which is why a cat may perfectly well be represented as a cloud of soft fur with claws. This is what the child has experienced cradling a cat in his arms, so this is the "reality" of the cat. A child shouldn't be reprimanded for leaving out legs or a tail. Such reprimands lead to avoidance of drawing in order to avoid being scolded again.

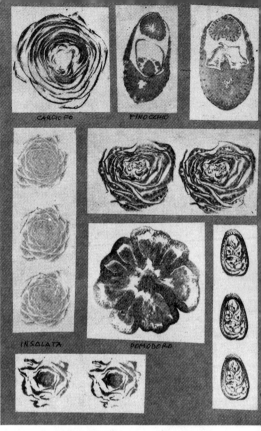

CARCIOFO

FINOCCHIO

INSALATA

POMODORO

A method like the present one, involving the use of sectioned plants as stamps, restores a child's confidence in expressing themselves in images. It strips away fears of making mistakes. Many vegetables lend themselves to this exercise with the lone exception of those that are too soft or watery: lettuce, celery, fennel, cabbage, onions, peppers, berries, flower stems, etc. The plant may be sectioned either vertically or horizontally or according to personal preferences, but the cut needs to leave a flat, uncurved surface.

BORRO

CAVOLFIORE

CIPOLLA

SEDANO

BACCHE DI FIORI

SEDANO

SEMI DI PITOSFORA

PREZZEMOLE

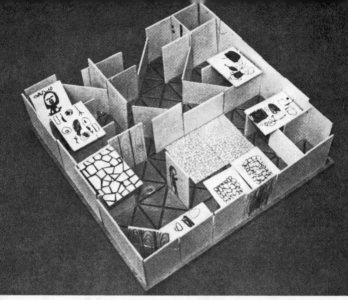

One game that simulates creativity is this
labyrinth. The child has at its disposal
a square plate whose sides each measure
thirty centimeters. Imprinted on this plate
is a grooved pattern containing smaller
squares crisscrossed by a diagonal grid.
There are also gray cards whose sides
match the size of each square or diagonal
slot which means that they can be inserted
into these perpendicular or diagonal
slots. Some of these cards have images
printed on them that allow for vertical or
horizontal insertion: leaves, rocks, gates,
bricks. Others are blank and can be used
as the child sees fit. The child selects the
cards he or she wishes and inserts them
upright in the selected slots. He or she is
free to draw on the blank cards as well
as to make use of those that bear printed
images. A labyrinth can be built, or the
floor plan of a home with its walls and
doors. Other small toys, like animals and
the like, can be introduced into the game
for purposes of creative play.

166

THREE-DIMENSIONAL GAMES

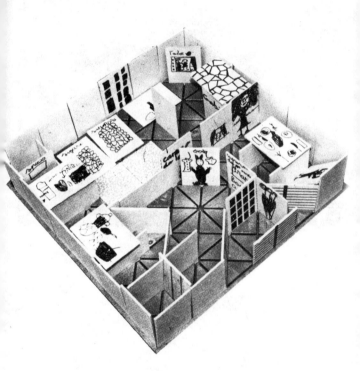

The two illustrations show the composition of a seven-year-old girl who built an apartment complete with everything from beds to bathrooms. She completed her project by means of drawings.

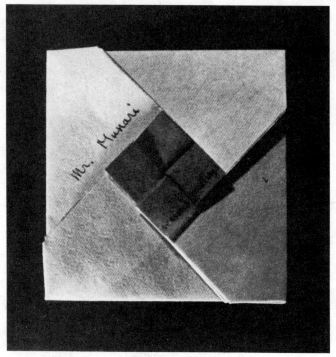

Sori Yanagi, colored two-sheet origami.[47]

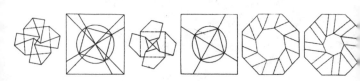

Some schemes for folding origami
developed by Sori Yanagi.

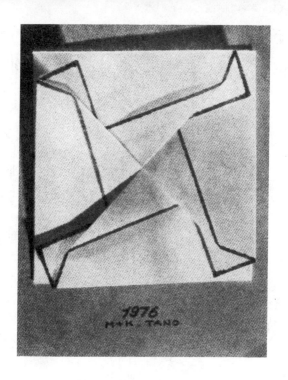

ORIGAMI

Origami is an ancient Japanese pastime
that results in the creation of animal
figures, flowers, or simply geometrical
figures by folding and refolding, without
any cuts, small sheets of colored paper.
The greatest master of origami was the
Japanese Uchiyama, who passed away
in 1969 and devoted more than half of
his life to inventing and making origami
through experiments in geometry and
topology.[48] Today, the young Sori Yanagi
is continuing his work because origami
contains principles that may be applicable
to design.

169

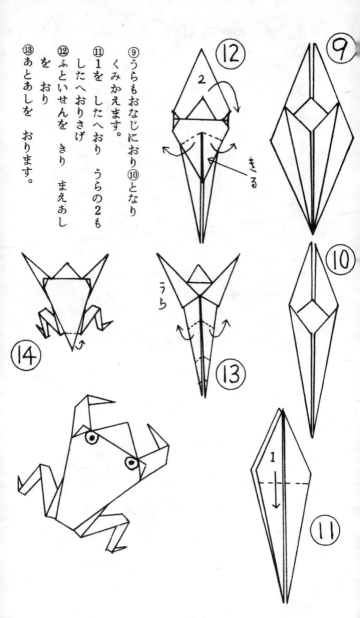

⑨ うらも おなじに おり ⑩ となり くみかえます。

⑪ 1を した へ おり うらの2も した へ おりさげ

⑫ ふといせんを きり まえあし を おり

⑬ あとあしを おります。

きる

うら

170

かえる

てんせんはやじるしのようにおります。

⑤てんせんのようなおりめを　よくつけて
⑥のようにおり　うらもおなじに
おります。⑦までは九十八頁のつる
とおなじです
⑦(あ)と(い)が　あわさるように　おり
うらもおなじにおって　くみかえます
⑧てんせんをやじるしのようにおります

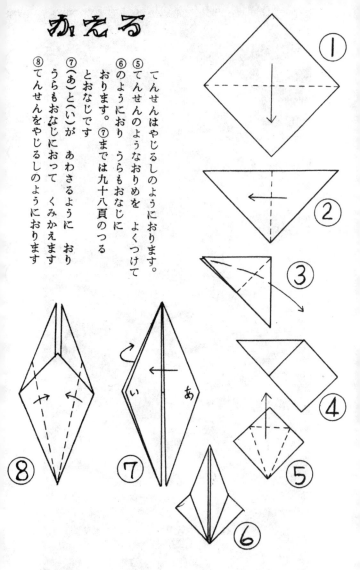

In Japanese elementary schools, children are taught to play by inventing and building origami figures. Children so trained develop a better sense of precision and know how to transform a two-dimensional sheet into a three-dimensional form with ease.

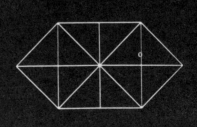

172

Structural games teach children geometrical forms that, to adults, seem complex. This sphere is made out of small, identical components that can be attached to one another following a simple rule.

THE ANALYSIS OF FORMS

A study of the forms contained within a given form. Some elements are extracted and others eliminated within an overall design composed of vertical, horizontal, and diagonal lines. In the process one becomes aware of the many varied designs contained within an overall structure. A creative exercise carried out by students at the School of Plastic Arts, Ljubljana, with Prof. Zoran Didek, in 1972.

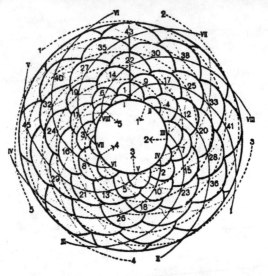

In his book *On Growth and Form*, D'Arcy Wentworth Thompson shows us how we can come to a better understanding of natural shapes by studying the process of their formation. Published in English in 1917 and in Italian in 1969, the book explains Thompson's research methods and provides many illustrated examples of his work. His is a method of inquiry and study that is closer in spirit to Asia than to Western approaches solely concerned with forms in themselves. Carried out with scientific rigor, the analysis is rich in objective facts: a model of how best to achieve genuine knowledge of the real. The conventional life drawings that are unimaginatively assigned in art schools could be better taught and understood if they were reimagined along the lines of Thompson.

Leonardo da Vinci himself studied nature by means of a scientific method. This implied not limiting himself to drawing what could be seen but instead investigating why that object had assumed a given shape. When he drew parts of the human body, he represented them as elements within a machine and each part, whether in tension or in compression, was rendered with precision and clarity. In some drawings muscles are represented as elastic bands in ways that reveal the body's overall operation. From these modes of research, he derived creative applications of what he had learned from reality.

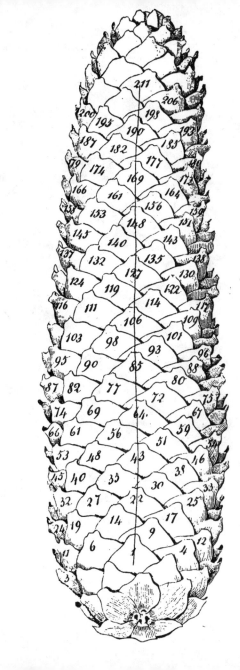

An example of two-dimensional modules
arranged into rotational symmetries.

COMBINABLE MODULE
IN STRUCTURED FIELDS[49]

Here's another exercise for stimulating creativity.
Sheets of paper printed with square or triangular
grids are required. Modules are designed on these
supports: closed shapes whose perimeter follows the
structure of the grid. These shapes can be drawn
either with straight lines or compass-drawn curves so
long as the vertex of every angle and edge touches
a point of intersection on the grid and every curve
has a center that is related to the grid. Modules with
varying shapes arise as a function of the personality of
their creator. Each creator will cut out four modules
(if the square grid has been chosen) or three modules
(if working with the triangular grid). The modules
are combined with one another, touching along their
edges in rotational symmetry without ever overlapping.
When one alters the point of contact, the overall form
of the four or three modules changes.

This experiment can be transposed into three
dimensions by folding the module according to the
angle of the structure from which it originated. In this
way one can achieve modular structures capable of
a great number of variations. This exercise promotes
understanding of the problems associated with the
modulation of space, with the prefabrication of
modular systems for decoration, installation design,
and architecture. Such solutions are common in the
pavilions encountered at major international expositions
because it's the most economical mode of construction
but can also accommodate many variations. The creator
proceeds following a logical method, devising a shape
and a compositional rule. The most ancient examples
of this procedure date back to Chinese, Islamic, and
Persian decoration.

Some writing systems from different cultures. From top to bottom: ancient Chinese, Sanskrit, Hamaric, Greek, Bengali, Hebrew, ancient Persian, Thai, Arabic, Japanese, Tibetan.

At his school in Vho, Italy, Mario Lodi transforms the question of studying the languages of humanity and, therefore, writing systems, into a game.[50] He asks children themselves to invent signs and helps them to build an alternate alphabet. The children then write texts with this alphabet. Here's a poem composed by Elena, reproduced from the fifth-grade newspaper *Insieme*.

Charles Cros, lunar writing from *Le caillou mort d'amour*, *Le chat noir* (March 20, 1886).[51]

Some fantasy alphabets, ancient and new.

Fantasy: a Gothic majuscule from the
seventeenth century.

NDS PAS ILLISIBLE NE LE RENDS
AS ILLISIBLE NE LE RENDS PAS IL
IBLE NE LE RENDS PAS ILLISIBLE
LE RENDS PAS ILLISIBLE NE LE
NDS PAS ILLISIBLE NE LE RENDS
AS ILLISIBLE NE LE RENDS PAS IL
SIBLE NE LE RENDS PAS ILLISIBLE
LE RENDS PAS ILLISIBLE NE LE
NDS PAS ILLISIBLE NE LE RENDS
AS ILLISIBLE NE LE RENDS PAS IL
SIBLE NE LE RENDS PAS ILLISIBLE
LE RENDS PAS ILLISIBLE NE LE
NDS PAS ILLISIBLE NE LE RENDS
AS ILLISIBLE NE LE RENDS PAS IL

Bifur, typeface designed by Cassandre for
the Fonderie Deberny & Peignot (1929).

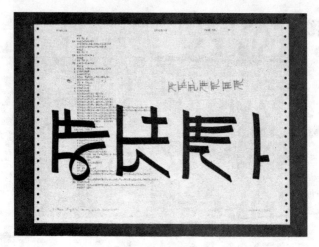

Bruno Munari, *Illegible Writing of an Unknown People*, 1973. Photo: Furia.

Giovanna Sandri, *This Is What Isi the Great Has Said: Let Someone, the Son of Someone, Li ve* (1975).[52] The creative use of an invented alphabet.

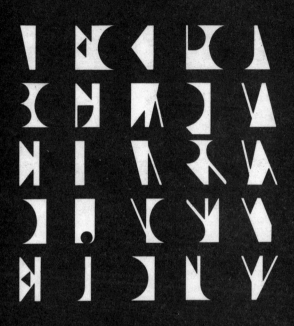

Pino Tovaglia, visualization of the
spacing between the letters of the alphabet
(1974).[53] Seen in this way, these spaces
present themselves as additional letters.
If so, how do they sound? Each space is
framed by two different letters.

GRAPHIS 103

Pino Tovaglia, cover of the review
Graphis (1960).
The author proposes an in-depth reading
of the word "graphis," superimposing
the letters that compose the word, one
on top of the other. The letters are cut
out of semitransparent paper. They are
sequenced in accord with reading order
translated into depth.

ROC-A

0 1 2 3 4 5 6 7 8 9

1428

0 1 2 3 4 5 6 7 8 9

7 B

0 1 2 3 4 5 6 7 8 9

NOF

0 1 2 3 4 5 6 7 8 9

Numbers designed by IBM for reading on
electronic calculators.

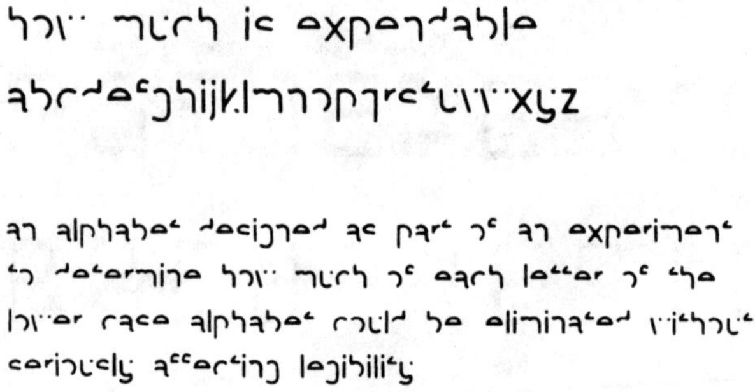

which word is expendable

abcdefghijklmnopqrstuvwxyz

an alphabet designed as part of an experiment
to determine how much word of each letter of the
lower case alphabet could be eliminated without
seriously affecting legibility

An experiment carried out by Brian Coe
to determine "how much of each letter of
the lower-case alphabet could be eliminated without seriously affecting legibility."[54]

Pino Tovaglia, graphic variations on
La Gioconda (1962). Various permutations
of four-color printing are on display
in this image. In each version of the
illustrious portrait the colors have
been altered in order to achieve highly
varied effects.

The famous Ryoan-ji garden in Kyoto,
Japan. The world's most celebrated
Zen garden, it was the final work of
an elderly gardener, built at the end of
the fourteenth century. We usually walk
through gardens composed of flower beds,
plants, and flowers. This garden, however,
is only for contemplation and is made up
of fine gravel and fifteen larger stones
composed in groups of two, three, five,
and five. These groupings are devised in
such a way as to ensure that every stone

FIFTEEN STONES

is always hiding another stone, irrespective of one's viewing position. The idea is that one knows that there are fifteen stones, but they can never be seen at the same time. This garden is the exact opposite of the most famous Italian gardens in which plants have been shaped into geometric forms: cubes, spheres, cones, or animal shapes. An infantile idea that projects what one knows onto what one doesn't and constricts plant forms without striving to understand them.

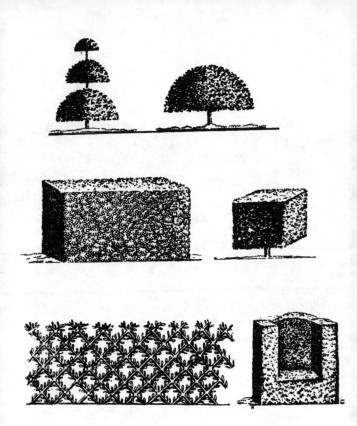

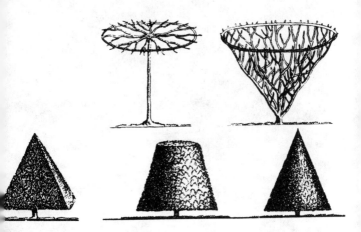

To sculpt plants in this fashion, to shape them into geometrical forms, is to misunderstand the natural form of plants. It's an expression of stupidity and arrogance, not of fantasy.

A straight bridge is considered banal in the Japanese landscape design, all the more so if it's a pedestrian bridge. An irregular bridge like this one is an expression of

fantasy that prompts many avenues of
thought. There's a Japanese rule that says,
"Perfection is beautiful but dumb; it needs
to be known but broken."

195

An India ink bottle designed at the first Bauhaus.[55] The form of the bottle is determined by its function and embraced as its logical form. During this era people still wrote with a dip pen and when the nib was dipped into standard vertical bottles, the handle would also get smeared with ink. A design solution of this kind makes sure the pen doesn't get wet. Thanks to its carefully studied form, it always provides the nib with the same quantity of ink and keeps the pen from dipping too far down into the ink well.

Moreover, an "inverted" bottle of this sort immediately stands out with respect to conventional bottles, so its function encompasses drawing attention in shop windows. In this case, its form is not a caprice of fantasy or the result of a desire for novelty or oddity, but the logical functional solution and is understood as such. During the same era there were plenty of fantasy bottles for sale—in the shape of a hand, a revolver, a woman's body, Garibaldi, a fish: designs we still encounter in antique stores.

AN INVENTED MUSEUM

A cluster of stains on the wall looked like an archipelago. To turn the wall of a small peasant home
in Panarea [the smallest of seven Aeolian Islands
north of Sicily] into a map of the archipelago, all
that was needed were labels with the names of the
islands. The names were part real and part made
up: Vulcano, Lipari, Dattilo, Basiluzzo, Panarea,
but because there were more than seven stains, we
added Panaruzzo, Liparea, Salinea, Stromboluzzo,
and so on to the real names. Alberto and I were
having a lot of fun and prompted by an interest in

197

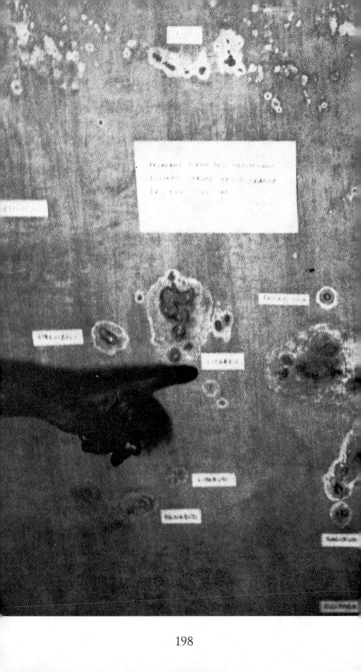

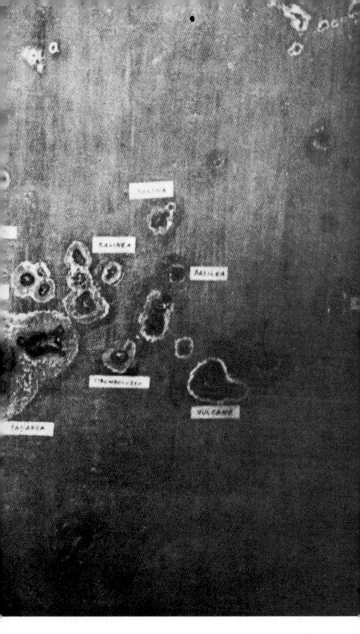

SALINA

SALINEA

BASILEA

STROMBOLI EAE

VULCANO

PANAREA

199

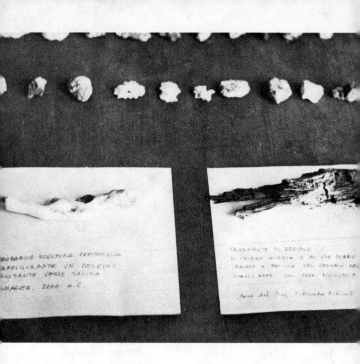

playing with further visual connections, we started studying the objects assembled in this small and nearly empty house.[56] We discovered that the cast-iron oven door could become a shield and a trowel could become a fighting stick, so we exhibited them is this manner. We began to think about inviting the friends who had joined us for this summer vacation in Panarea to the inauguration of our on-site Invented Museum. We discovered a rounded wood fragment which the locals used as a float before they discovered pumice. We found a putative statue of the wife of one of the fishermen (in reality, the dry root of a caper bush). We uncovered a rusted Aeolian chastity belt with two perforations. We discovered a wood sculpture that appeared to

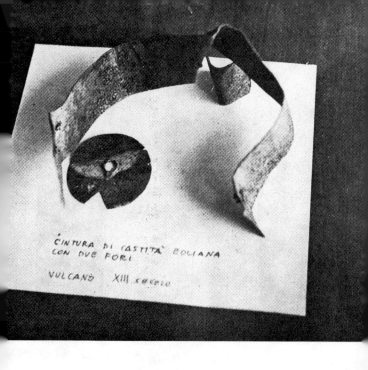

CINTURA DI CASTITA' EOLIANA
CON DUE FORI

VULCANO XIII secolo

portray a dolphin. We uncovered a fragment of a
pirate's wooden peg leg about the size of a pencil
which allowed us, in turn, to reconstruct the life-size
pirate by means of a drawing of a blank sheet
that began with the placement of the fragment
in the proper location. (This was the beginning of
my *Theoretical Reconstructions of Imaginary Objects*
series.)[57] We also discovered an infinite number of
residual fragments of unknown origin and usage on
the beach facing Stromboluzzo. These were presented
as a donation from Professor Filicudo Filicudi, the
sponsor of the Invented Museum.[58]
On the evening of the inauguration, before sunset
(because there wasn't any electricity in Panarea at the
time), we invited our friends to visit the museum.

SASSO LIGNEO

USATO DAGLI INDIGENI
COME GALLEGGIANTE
PRIMA DELLA SCOPERTA
DELLA POMICE.

LIPARI · 1500 a C. marzo

Professor Filicudo Filicudi sent along a note written
on a fig leaf stating that he was unable to attend
but had sent his personal pair of scissors to cut
the ribbon.
Our friends admired the museum, Piero de Biasi[59]
took photographs, some local wine was consumed
and almonds from the tree that was at the door of
the museum were eaten. Evening fell and everyone
lit their flashlights and conversed late into the night.
Caper bush flowers open after dark, and the air was
fragrant with their scent.
The next day we had to dismantle the museum
because tourists were showing up, convinced that it
was real.

To understand that an object can also be another object is a form of knowledge that is associated with mutations. Mutations are reality's sole constant: everything changes (as has been said by many).[60] Widespread in China, the game known as Tangram helps to accustom children to this truth: it's a square table divided into seven elements that can be recombined in infinite ways and forms. The base object remains always the same: a square made up of seven parts. The images it generates are infinite.

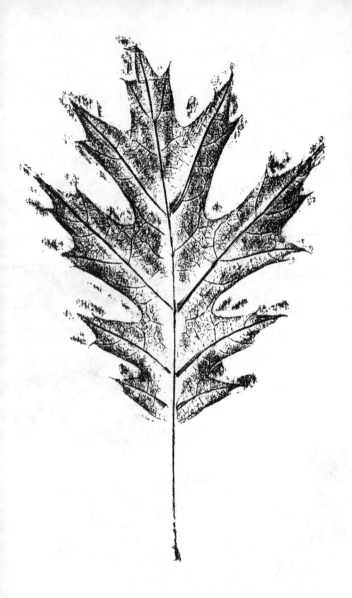

The imprint of an oak leaf.

FROM ONE THING IS BORN ANOTHER[61]

A leaf can also become the source of an exploration
that exposes otherwise hidden relationships. Suppose
that we make a print of an oak leaf like this one.
We overlay a semitransparent sheet over the print
and mark the leaf's contours. On another sheet we
transcribe only the major veins. On another sheet we
indicate only its outermost points. On another sheet
we mark only the innermost portions of its contours.
On another sheet we trace the lines connecting
the outermost points and... on another sheet... we
can them layer them, two or three at a time, and
discover so many different patterns, all generated on
the basis of the same leaf.

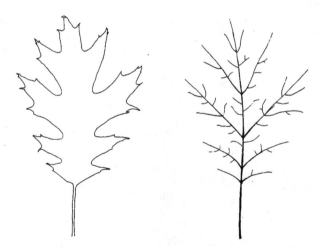

The contours of an oak leaf.

The veins of an oak leaf.

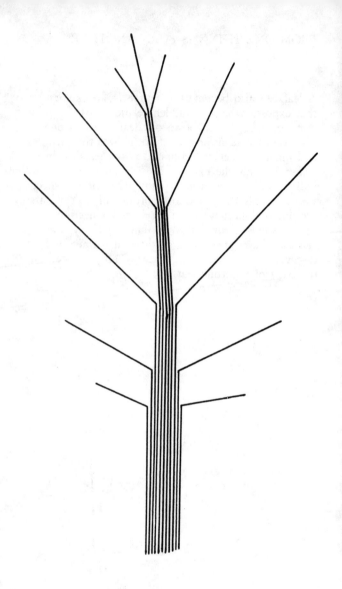

The main veins that connect the outermost extensions of the leaf to the stem.

The key junctures in the vein structure
of the leaf.

The outermost points of the leaf, its tips.

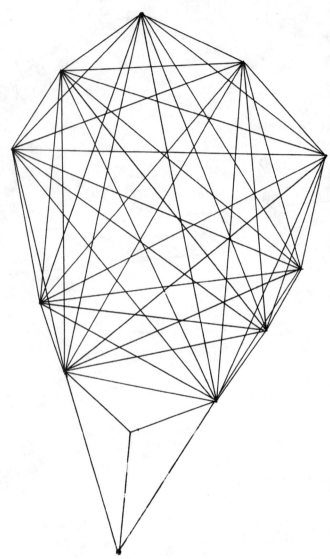

The relationship between all the outermost points of the leaf.

208

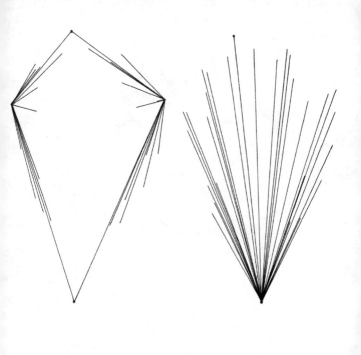

The relationship of the outermost points of the leaf on its right and left sides.

The relationship of the outermost points of the leaf with its base.

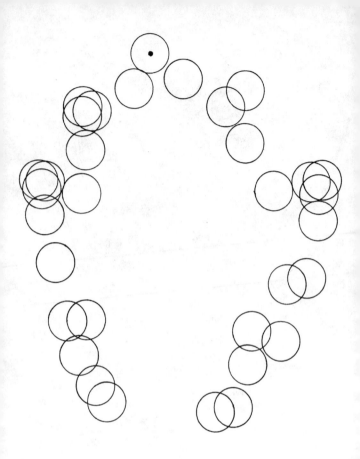

Circles of equal radius drawn around the outermost points of the leaf.

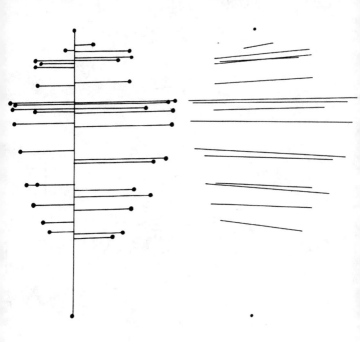

Lateral connections between the outermost points of the leaf and its central axis.

Connections between the outermost points of the leaf of the same variety.

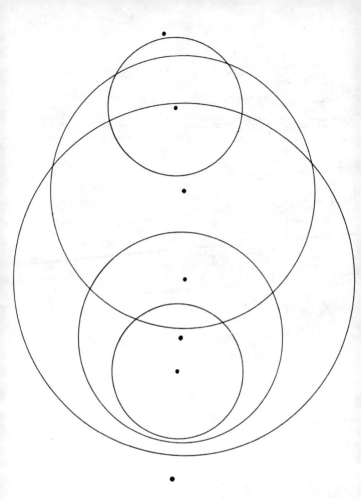

Circles whose center lies along the central
axis of the leaf whose radius is determined
by the vein structures.

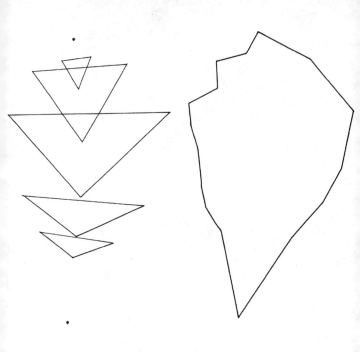

The relationship between the outermost points of the leaf and the points of attachment of the veins to the central axis.

The leaf's maximum footprint.

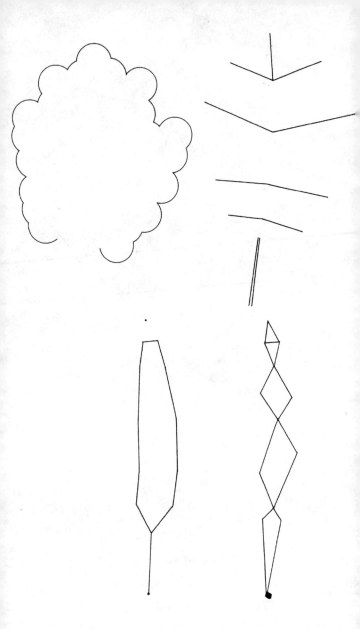

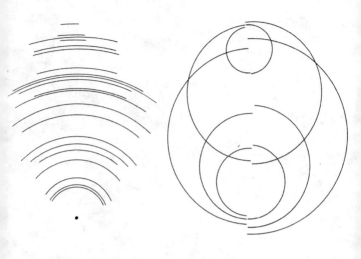

Free variations on the same leaf. Every line and every curve that has been drawn refers to the measurements of the original leaf. The compass can be aligned with the outermost points and the radius of the circle determined by other constants. The straight lines can connect and conjoin all the points along the innermost contours of the leaf or alternate between inner and outer points. Other points yet to be discovered can be connected by means of curves and lines...

All the drawings from these last pages can be superimposed, one on top of the other, as you see fit. This is because the placement of every mark remains anchored in the physical structure of the original oak leaf. The variations are personal and infinite.

215

A game of transparent overlays entertains a
group of children. It's a game that unfolds
at the speed of thought. The children have
fun putting images together and taking
them apart. More than a billion combinations are possible.

INDEX

Notes (2024)

Jeffrey Schnapp

1   Mario de Biasi (1923-2013) was a celebrated Italian photojournalist whose collaboration with the magazine *Epoca* lasted over three decades and included the coverage of such momentous events as the Hungarian uprising of 1956. In 2006, the city of Milan awarded him its highest honor: the Ambrogino d'oro. Several of his photographs are present in *Fantasy*, in which he is described as being "known for his experiments with new ways of creating images that employ simple procedures."

2   As is often the case, Munari's examples are directly drawn from his work experiences or creative practice. In 1936, he designed publicity panels including paint samples for the Colorificio Italiano MaxMeyer for the section of the VI Triennale di Milano dedicated to construction systems and building materials (installation by Giuseppe Pagano and Guido Frette). Subsequently—and apparently stretching into the 1950s—he designed packaging for the Industria Vernici Italiane's industrial enamel division, color catalogs for IRC, and advertising posters for the printing ink company Colorgraf. (Sketches of all may be found in the collection of the Fondazione Massimo and Sonia Cirulli in Bologna.)

3   The phrasing echoes the title of Munari's subse-quent volume (and of one of the concluding chapters of the present volume): *Da cosa nasce cosa. Appunti per una metodologia progettuale*, first published by Laterza in 1981. Much like the present book, *Da cosa nasce cosa* demonstrates not just how "one thing leads to the next" but also how the methodical character of the processes give birth to new objects and ideas.

4   Munari has in mind the Thomas Horn Engineering London-built steam engine, dating from circa 1850, that is on display in the galleries of the Leonardo

da Vinci Museum of Science and Technology. The engine in question is built around a stout Doric column. An image is available at https://commons.wikimedia.org/wiki/File:Macchina_vapore_Horn_Museo_scienza_e_tecnologia_Milano.jpg.

5   Alberto Munari (1940–2021) was Bruno's son, a noted psychologist and researcher. He was also the student, collaborator, and successor of Jean Piaget at the International Center for Genetic Epistemology in Geneva, Switzerland. Alberto went on to found (with his wife Donata Fabbri) the Laboratori di Epistemologia Operativa that were widely adopted for training purposes in schools, public institutions, and private corporations. Alberto's work helped to shape his father's design laboratories for children.

6   Munari's interest in patents translated into filings to protect his own inventions on numerous occasions: in 1954 he applied for (and received) a patent for his folding paper sunglasses; in the mid-1950s (with Pirelli) for the bendable *gatto Meo* and *scimmietta Zizì*; in 1962 for the Cubo ashtray; and in the early 1980s for a "snap fastening handle for pots" (held by his client Lagostina).

7   Although the reference is unspecific, Munari is clearly thinking about his own works for Pirelli, his own and Enzo Mari's designs for Danese, and the sorts of toys that designers such as Charles and Ray Eames had been developing for Creative Playthings in Princeton, New Jersey.

8   A photojournalist by training, Jacqueline Vodoz (1921–2005), co-founded the Danese Milano company with Bruno Danese, with which Munari collaborated closely over the course of several decades.

9   Based on ideas stretching back to ancient festivities like the Saturnalia and forward to contemporary carnivals, the "world upside-down" motif was popularized in nineteenth-century Catalan *aucas* and Castillian *aleluyas*, grids of vignettes that were sometimes cut up and transformed into playing cards. Munari is apparently alluding to these popular precursors of modern comics.

10   During the years 1933–48 Munari developed close to a hundred sculptural assemblages that he referred to as "useless machines." Less a critique of mechanical utility than experiments with materials and motion, they typically involve the suspension of light materials in a dynamic setting where the balance between the elements undergoes constant change.

11   Though I have translated the word *fatto* (*il lettore visuale poteva seguire un fatto visivo*) as "plot," the literal translation is "fact." The word suggests that it is the very facticity or materiality of the book that constitutes its narrative structure.

12   *Libro illegibile N.Y. 1*, (Milan: Lucini, 1967) was commissioned by the Museum of Modern Art in New York and developed in the spring of 1967 when Munari was a visiting professor at the program in Visual and Environmental Studies at Harvard University.

13   The book in question goes by the title of *An Unreadable Quadrat-Print* and was printed by Steendrukkerij de Jong & Co in Hillversum in 1953 in a numbered edition of 2000 copies. Thirty-six pages in length, 25 × 25 cm in format, it contains an inner (bound) booklet covered by a larger orthogonally folded sheet with an autobiography handwritten in multiple languages.

14 Noburo Muramoto (1920–1995) was a follower of
Georges Ohsawa, the founding father of macrobi-
otics, and dedicated himself to its dissemination of
Asian medical thought over the course of a career
that included the publication of several books
of lectures, including *Healing Ourselves: A Book
to Serve as a Companion in Time of Illness and
Health,* (New York: Avon Books, 1972).

15 Fulvio Bianconi (1915–1996) was a celebrated
postwar Italian graphic designer but is also remembered for his pioneering works in Murano glass.

16 The volume was originally published in 1972 with
Harper and Row; Munari is referring to the Italian
translation published by Garzanti.

17 Roberto Lanterio was a graphic artist with whom
Munari collaborated during the period of the
writing of *Fantasy.* The author of *Disegnare una
casa* (Bologna: Zanichelli, 1979), Lanterio was also
associated with Mario Lodi's review *A&B—Adulti e
bambini che vogliono diventare amici.*

18 These works are among Munari's most remembered and were originally published as a suite
of photographs in *Domus* 332 (July 1957) as
Le forchette parlanti di Munari (Munari's Talking
Forks). Reworked as a book of ink drawings in 1958
entitled *Le forchette di Munari* (Munari's Forks),
the forks included a wide array of gestures from
greetings to expressions of disapproval. During
this same period, Munari had competed in the
Reed and Barton Design Competition for Italy,
centered on the design of place settings.

19 As is clear in Munari's text, the entire passage
is playing with the fact that the Italian word for
brush is *pennello,* a masculine noun. The suffix

-essa transforms it into a feminine noun, narrows the word's semantic field to flat brushes, and calls attention to other "feminine" attributes of the object that might otherwise remain invisible. An additional ambiguity hovering in the background of this transformation of a masculine paintbrush into a *pennellessa* may be the fact that the Italian word for penis (*pene*) is itself evocative of *pennello*.

20 Munari's own chromatic variations on the tale of *Little Red Riding Hood*, starting with *Cappuccetto verde* (Turin: Einaudi, 1972), are obvious instances of this facet of fantasy at work: the story was reworked in green, yellow, blue, and white, often with variations in the illustrative techniques employed. These variations were collected in the volume *Cappuccetto rosso verde giallo blu e bianco* (Turin: Einaudi, 1997).

21 The reference is to Jacques Carelman, *Catalogue d'objets introuvables et cependant indispensables aux personnes telles que acrobates, ajusteurs, amateurs d'art, alpinistes* (Balland: Paris, 1969); the English translation appeared in 1971 from Ballantine Books.

22 Munari is, of course, referring to Hans Christian Andersen's celebrated folktale "The Emperor's New Clothes."

23 The allusion is to James Whale's science fiction horror film starring Claude Rains, Gloria Stuart, and William Harrigan. Based on H. G. Wells's 1897 novel *The Invisible Man*, the film was remade in 2020 (dir. Leigh Whannell).

24 As he readily admits, Munari's recollection of the passage from Alphonse Allais is inaccurate. Captain Cap is talking not about himself but rather about

a Californian who performs on a slide trombone made of wicker. Instead of making use of sheet music in the standard fashion, the Californian performs to birds trained to distribute themselves with precision along telegraph lines. The five telegraph lines represent the lines on a musical staff. Each bird represents a single note. The bird's color is indicative of the duration of each note. Upon arriving at the place of performance, the Californian frees up his birds to form the score that he is about to perform. See Allais, "Dressage," in *Deux et deux font cinq* (*Oeuvres Posthumes*) (Paris: Ollendorff, 1895).

25   Munari most likely has in mind such paintings as *Furniture in the Valley* (1927) and *The Return of Ulysses* (1968) which show the ancient hero rowing across a sea in a modern bedroom.

26   The passage refers to Buster Keaton's 1924 *Sherlock Jr.*, the film which immediately preceded his transition to stardom in *The Navigator* (1924).

27   *Hellzapoppin'* was a 1941 film adaptation of the Broadway musical of that same name directed by H. C. Potter for Universal Pictures; the film is remembered for its surreal comedy and playful violations of fourth wall conventions.

28   The author is alluding to the celebrated scene from Charlie Chaplin's *The Gold Rush* (1925) in which he cooks and eats a boot with fellow prospector Big Jim McKay.

29   The hat in question is that of a *bersagliere*: the extravagant, black capercaillie-feather–crested, wide-brimmed hat worn by members of the top marksmen in the Italian Army's infantry corps.

30   Known in Italy as *il re della risata* (the king of laugh-
     ter), "Ridolini," alias Lawrence Semon (1889–1928),
     was one of the most celebrated American comic
     actors of the silent cinema, remembered in
     particular for collaborations with Stan Laurel
     and Oliver Hardy (before the two joined forces).
     Influenced by his early work as a cartoonist,
     Semon's films were influential during the silent
     era. In Italy his work underwent a postwar renais-
     sance when his syndicator sold his comedies
     to Italian television where they were reworked
     with a soundtrack and voice-over by the comedian
     Tino Scotti. Munari has in mind Semon's use of
     tricks such as rocking the camera to alter the
     horizons of the picture plane.

31   On the history of the Monte Olimpino studio and
     Munari's collaborations on experimental cinema
     projects, see Marcello Piccardo, *La collina del
     cinema* (Como: Nodo Libri, 1992).

32   The examples refer to two famous experiments with
     stroboscopic photography carried out by Harold
     Eugene Edgerton at the Massachusetts Institute for
     Technology in the mid-twentieth century.

33   The making of *Tempo nel tempo* is thoroughly
     discussed in pp. 36–45 of Piccardo, *La collina del
     cinema*.

34   *Them!* (1954) starred James Whitmore and was
     directed by Gordon Douglas. *Tarantula!* (1955)
     starred John Agar and was directed by Jack Arnold,
     and is yet another sci-fi story of research spinning
     out of control: a miracle nutrient meant to save the
     world is ingested by a test tarantula who grows
     to titanic proportions. Both are, in one sense or
     another, "nuclear monster" films.

35 The film referred to is *The Incredible Shrinking Man* (1957) directed by the same director as *Tarantula!* It was based on the 1956 sci-fi novel by Richard Matheson, *The Shrinking Man*.

36 Munari's reference is to the 1966 sci-fi film *Fantastic Voyage*, directed by Richard Fleischer and starring Stephen Boyd, Arthur Kennedy, Edmond O'Brien, Donald Pleasence, and Raquel Welch.

37 The original film, directed by Kurt Neumann, was released in 1958; two sequels would follow (*Return of the Fly* [1959] and *Curse of the Fly* [1965]), as well as David Cronenberg's celebrated 1986 remake.

38 The reference is to Lon Chaney Jr. who, alongside Beverly Garland, starred in Roy del Ruth's *The Alligator People* (1959).

39 Perhaps relevant to this passage are Munari's own subsequent playful unmaskings of the mystique of painting in the *Olii su tela* (Oil on Canvas) series (1980): unstretched canvases (of hemp, linen, and cotton) daubed in various oils (castor, linseed, almond, poppyseed, olive) and exhibited in an art gallery.

40 The subject of Munari's book *Disegnare un albero* (Bologna: Zanichelli, 1978), translated as *Drawing a Tree* (Mantova: Corraini Edizioni, 1984).

41 "Direct" projections of transparent, semitransparent, and opaque materials compacted into slide frames were integral to Munari's artwork going back to the early 1950s. These works were first exhibited in Milan at Studio B 24 in 1953 and subsequently, in 1954–55, at the Museum of Modern Art, New York.

42   It is worth noting that, as he explains later in this
     section, Munari is referring to *glass* slides of the
     sort that were still frequent in mid-century, even
     as the transition to 35 mm Kodachrome type slides
     was well underway. Not unlike some slides for
     microscopes today, these slides were composed
     of two hinged glass squares attached to a metallic
     frame with a small clip on the open end of the frame
     that allowed you to insert 2D materials between
     the glass panes (including 35 mm images), and then
     quickly snap the slide together and slot it into a
     standard projector or projector slide tray. Such
     slides are referred to as *vetrini* in Italian: a word
     that recalls not only the word for glass (*vetro*)
     but also for the display windows of department
     stores (*vetrine*).

43   The passage is less a self-critique than a clarifi-
     cation. Munari's pre-World War I career largely
     developed within the fold of Futurism and, from
     the outset, he shared much of the movement's
     heroic vision of the civilization of machines,
     from automobiles to aviation, and participated in
     such key exhibitions as the *Mostra di 34 futuristi*,
     Galleria Pesaro, Milan (1927); *Futuristi italiani*,
     XVII Biennale di Venezia (1930); *Prampolini et les
     aeropeintres futuristes italiens*, Galerie de la
     Reinassance, Paris (1932); *Mostra dell'aeropittura
     e della pittura dei futuristi italiani*, XVIII Biennale di
     Venezia (1932); and Mostra dell'aeronautica, Milan
     (1934). Temperamentally more of an ironist and
     cartoonist than a devotee of "high art," his work in
     the 1930s increasingly split off two-dimensional
     work, whether artistic or commercial, from properly
     kinetic experiments like his sculptural "useless
     machines." By the postwar period, he had distanced
     himself from these Futurist debts and beginnings,
     reducing his Futurist biography to a fleeting
     reference to the "useless machines" (dating them

to 1930) and then jumping to his children's books of 1945 in what became his standard autobiography.

44 Munari's datings are sometimes approximate and the artistic prank referred to in the image probably dates from 1945 (not 1940 as indicated in *Fantasy*). The bottle form suggests not a bottle of mint liqueur but rather mint syrup of the sort sold to this day in bottles with sinuous waists by Fabbri 1905 in Bologna, Italy.

45 Once again, the argument of Munari, *Disegnare un albero* (Bologna: Zanichelli, 1978).

46 Like several other sections of *Fantasy*, this one was spun off in 1982 as the pamphlet/book *Rose nell'insalata* (Turin: Einaudi, 1982); an English translation was published as *Roses in the Salad* (Mantua: Corraini, 2004).

47 Munari got to know Sori Yanagi in the course of one of his trips to Japan. Remembered for such creations as the "butterfly stool," Yanagi (1915–2011) was a prominent industrial designer whose work managed to combine traditional Japanese craft practices with international modernism.

48 There are several imprecisions here. The true master of modern origami is widely considered to be Akira Yoshizawa (1911–2005) not Kosho Uchiyama, to whom Munari is referring. A Buddhist priest who, unlike Yoshizawa, made use of cutting in some of his designs, Uchiyama authored a variety of books on origami, including *Origami Zukan*, for children. Born in 1912, he died in 1998, not 1969.

49 Munari's longstanding interest in modular, recursive, and generative mathematical structures is reflected in such projects as his abstract "Peano

curve" paintings and prints from the 1970s, which explore Giuseppe Peano's groundbreaking work on space-filling curves.

50   Mario Lodi (1922–2014) was one of the great reformers of the Italian elementary school system, remembered for his emphasis on learner-centered education, the agency of children, and the role of storytelling and creative exercises. Long associated with the elementary school in his native town of Vho, he won the LEGO Foundation Prize in 1989 and went on to establish the Casa delle Arti e del Gioco in Drizzona (Cremona).

51   The source of this otherwise recondite reference is indicative of Munari's reading habits. Published by Jean-Jacques Pauvert, *Bizarre* was close to Surrealist and pataphysical currents on the French literary-artistic scene. Issue 32–33 (1964) was titled *Littérature illettrée ou la littérature à la lettre* (Illiterate Literature or Literature Taken Literally), and is entirely devoted to calligrams, concrete poetry, lettrism, and imaginary alphabets. The passage from Cros is found in Noël Arnaud's essay "Les jargons."

52   Giovanna Sandri (1923–2002) was a member of the Concrete art movement in which Munari himself also participated actively, remembered for her 1960s and '70s experiments with visual poetry, graphics, and collage.

53   Giuseppe Tovaglia (1923–1977) was a leading Milanese graphic artist who cultivated strong affinities with contemporary Swiss graphics as associated with figures like Max Bill. In 1972, with Munari, Bob Noorda, and Roberto Sambonet, he designed the logo for the region of Lombardy which is employed to this day.

54 Munari probably came upon this work in typograph-
   ical and design journals, like *Typographica* and
   Visible Language, reporting on ongoing research on
   the limits of legibility. Such work was associated not
   just with Brian Coe, but also with Herbert Spencer
   and Linda Reynolds.

55 Designed by the German architect and industrial
   designer Wilhelm Wagenfeld (1900–1990), the
   Pelikan ink bottle actually dates from 1938.
   Wagenfeld had studied at the Weimar Bauhaus
   and went on to direct the Dessau Bauhaus metal-
   working department in 1928. In 1938, at the time
   of the development of the Pelikan ink bottle,
   he occupied the position of artistic director at
   the United Lausitzer Glass Works in Weisswasser,
   Germany.

56 A reference to Munari's son, the psychologist
   Alberto Munari.

57 Munari's *Ricostruzione teoriche di un oggetto
   immaginario* (Theoretical Reconstructions of
   Imaginary Objects) were a series of works,
   mostly from the 1970s, that assumed the form
   of collages and mixed media work, as well as
   silkscreen prints, built around the playful handling
   of leftover materials.

58 Filicudi is, of course, one of the actual Aeolian
   islands (unlike Stromboluzzo which is one of the
   imaginative additions).

59 "Piero de Biasi" is doubtless the photographer
   Mario de Biasi, cited numerous times elsewhere
   in the volume.

60 The reference is to the ancient Greek philoso-
   pher Heraclitus of Ephesus who is said to have

proclaimed change (ῥεῖ rei [flux] or χωρέω choreo [movement]) as the signature of life itself.

61   As noted earlier, the title (as well as the chapter's argument) anticipates that of the subsequent volume *Da cosa nasce cosa. Appunti per una metodologia progettuale*.

The Method

Jeffrey Schnapp

"Everybody knows a different Munari."

With this phrase the prolific artist-designer sought to put a bow on his standard bio and tease future biographers. The phrase routinely arrived at the end of a sequence that began with "The Munari born in Milan in 1907," followed by an inventory of major and minor works ("The one who made the *Useless Machines* of 1930," "The one who made the *Illegible Books* of 1949," etc.), capped off by a verbal snapshot of the Munari-of-the-moment like, "the one who started children's workshops in museums in 1977."[i]

Rather than completeness or predictability, Munari's autobiography sought to drive home the point that life stories, career paths, and bodies of work are combinatory structures. From one thing is born another and then another still. The generative chain that leads from one thing to the next, however, isn't necessarily linear or causal, particularly when humanity taps into its deeper powers of imaginative concatenation. More than a timeline, a lifetime can just as easily be repre-sented, not to mention lived, as a zigzag, a scatterplot, an inward or outward rotating spiral, a grid of striated lines, or all the above.

First published in 1977, *Fantasy: Invention, Creativity, and Imagination in Visual Communication* explores this universe of combinatory possibilities.[ii] Its author was fresh on the heels of a decade of experiments with xerographic techniques that reflect the commitments he had accrued within the fold of the Concrete and Programmed art movements: in particular, an abiding interest in the generation of textures, elemental geometries (lines, grids, and patterns), and recursive systems and structures (like Giuseppe Peano's space-filling curves). The shift to xerography was undergirded by the same desacralizing and democratizing approach to design practice and artistic creation articulated in the publication that documents Munari's participation in the 1970 Venice Biennale:

If one seeks to develop an art that truly belongs to everyone (and not an "art for everyone," as one celebrated French critic recently proposed), it's necessary to find instruments that facilitate artistic creation and, at the same time, provide the methods and the training that creation implies. Great Art, a bourgeois construct, hand-made by Geniuses strictly for the ultra-rich, makes no sense in the present era. "Art for everyone" is just a low-cost version of Great Art, carrying forward the cult of genius while reinforcing the inferiority complex felt by most.

The technological possibilities of our era allow everyone to shape and craft aesthetic objects of aesthetic value. They permit those who have overcome their inferiority complex with respect to art to set their long-thwarted creativity to work.

One of the resulting responsibilities borne by contemporary visual practitioners is that of experimenting, finding and sharing the right instruments, passing along the "trade secrets" that support processes of making. Rank Xerox's machines can help anyone and everyone to express themselves. Invented to reproduce images, today they are capable of producing images.[iii]

Democratization and human-machine collaboration are the driving forces behind a methodical revitalization of contemporary design culture. But they are never tantamount to deskilling: even the freshly unencumbered citizen-designer requires the guidance of an experienced experimenter in the field of visual communication in order to forge works of genuine aesthetic value. Whether the tool in question is a photocopier, a brush, or a stick of charcoal, tools have rules. And even if such rules are designed to be broken, there's a difference between meaningful and meaningless, fresh and hackneyed forms of rule-breaking.

Fantasy sets out to untangle the complexities of rule-bound rule-breaking at a key transition in the mature, closing phase of Munari's career, from art and design *practice* to art and design *education*. It's no accident that its year of publication coincides with the staging of the first of his workshops for children, held at Milan's Pinacoteca di Brera, in which participants were invited to engage in creative exercises in dialogue with artworks from the past. Initiatives of this kind, later trademarked as Munari-Method Laboratories (*Laboratori metodo Munari*), became a constant from the Brera event through the time of Munari's passing in 1998. Some twenty are documented yet many more took place. They bore titles such as Hands That See (*Mani che guardano*), Playing With Art (*Giocare con l'arte*), Playing With Nature (*Giocare con la natura*), Playing With Photocopiers (*Giocare con la fotocopiatrice*), Playing With Staplers (*Giocare con la puntatrice*), and Tactile Tables (*Tavole tattili*). A variation was developed for senior citizens under the rubric of Rediscovering Childhood (*Ritrovare l'infanzia*). Several of these initiatives find their way into books published in the *Playing with Art* publication series that Munari edited for the publisher Zanichelli. Others were more ephemeral. Both the events and the documentary publications carried on after Munari's death thanks to the efforts of his son Alberto (Jean Piaget's successor at the International Center for Genetic Epistemology in Geneva, Switzerland), Donata Fabbri (Alberto's colleague and wife), Silvana Sperati, and their collaborators. Though hard to measure, the impact of the Munari-Method Laboratories on contemporary arts education, particularly in southern Europe, has proved enduring.

Every one of the human faculties cited in the present book's title—fantasy, invention, creativity, imagination— suggests an absence of constraint. Rather than method, they imply processes that are spontaneous, improvisatory, unplanned (and even unplannable). The boundary lines that distinguish one from the other appear blurred to the point of standing in the way of rigorous conceptualization. Where and when does creativity give way to imagination, imagination to invention, invention to creativity? Are they redundant? Is fantasy the overarching category within which the others are nested, as the book's title implies, or is the nest, at best, a messy affair? Then there's the problem of mixing. Human faculties tend to work in combination: is there a way to sort out how and when they operate in sequence or separately?

Munari tackles these challenges with pragmatism and eclecticism. He confronts them as someone who is neither a logician nor a cognitive scientist but instead a practitioner "who continuously relies upon these faculties in every professional endeavor" (7). He sketches out definitions and distinctions, tracks their genealogy on the basis of precedents culled from popular culture, art history, and contemporary art, and draws from his own experience in the studio, categorically refusing to trace a firm line between his commercial and non-commercial work. Most of all, Munari tests out his ideas in his "laboratories" for children understood as places of exploration and labor that conjoin the head to the hand, the act of thinking to the act of making. The goal isn't a new theory of creativity or a radical new method of art education. It's more modest: to explore what he refers to as the "fundamental constants" of how fantasy, invention, and creativity actually operate. In so doing, his aims are explicit: to promote creativity as a civic value, to combat pedagogies that stand in the way of children becoming full-fledged creative citizens, to clear a path for future systematic and comprehensive studies.

How does fantasy function according to Munari's account? Through the making of connections. Connections have their rules or, rather, they have a standard set of protocols that govern which combinations are most likely to be valid, significant, provocative, effective, or productive—a "grammar" so to speak. The grammar in question is eminently teachable, "otherwise, all this would be a purely subjective exercise, self-referential in nature, useful perhaps only for purposes of experimentation or research" (118). Much of *Fantasy* is dedicated to exploring these combinatory principles. They include reversals of the expected order of things like the literary topos of the "world upside down": the dunce crowned as king, the cart that leads the horse, Antipodeans who walk on their heads, landscapes that hover above the clouds. Other connections are built around principles of functional affinity (the "head" of a river, the "leg" of a table); substitutions in color, weight, material, or size (an indigo wedding cake, a Styrofoam sledgehammer, a glass automobile, a titanic tube of toothpaste); the incorporation of multiple heterogeneous elements within a single object (a Rube Goldberg machine, a hundred-headed Hydra, a cyborg); or dislocation (an underwater classroom, a ski resort in the desert). After inventorying such foundational modes of establishing meaningful connections, Munari concludes with some brief reflections on the forging of connections between connections. Here fantasy sets to work anchoring a now lighter-than-air floating glass automobile to the ambergris-scented leg of a table in the form of a bear's paw or imagining our cyborg as a 300-meter-tall monster ravaging the Manhattan skyline as it munches drones as if they were gnats.

There are two main foes when it comes to flexing the mental muscles Munari identifies with fantasy. The first is a lack of knowledge. Invention, creativity, and imagination work with information. Every human being contains within them a sort of multisensory database and it is within this database that fantasy carries out its operations. If that database is impoverished or corrupted, so will be the resulting outputs. The more one knows about the world, the more one can make creative associations and connections. So, children need to be exposed to as much information about the world as possible, even when memorization is involved. But they need to engage with that information in an active fashion. Quantity of data alone is no guarantee: to memorize large bodies of information can amount to little more than becoming the human double of "a dictionary that contains all the words with which one composes poems but not a single actual poem" (35). A higher faculty is required: the ability to forge connections ... the more connections, the better. That faculty is fantasy.

The second adversary is the commonplace notion that, rather than a corpus of teachable though open-ended tools and techniques, art is a form of free expression. Munari notes with dismay how teachers, particularly at the kindergarten and primary school level, envisage their art assignments as "free," even though that supposed "freedom" is constrained by the choice of traditional media such as paint, clay, and other conventional materials, and by the enforcement, implicit or explicit, of naturalistic canons. No technical training or information is offered regarding the tools that have been supplied: their powers, limitations, and affordances. Uniformity results. Instead of exercising their imagination or playing with the media being employed, children operate within the bounds of convention. They draw and paint what they have already seen or already know: faces, fields, flowers, houses, mountains, the sun, the moon.

The remedy for both ills is (properly structured) creative play. Here Munari's ruminations are informed by a rich vein of practical and theoretical thinking regarding childhood education and development that stretches back into the early twentieth century to figures like Maria Montessori. *Fantasy* makes explicit reference to the work of a variety of researchers from Alberto Munari and Donata Fabbri's team at the University of Geneva, to Edward de Bono (the Maltese physician and advocate of teaching processes of think-ing), to Rudolph Arnheim (*Visual Thinking*), to Mario Lodi (the activist reformer who sought to democratize Italian elementary school education in the 1960s and 1970s). Somewhere in the mix there are traces of the theories of Jean Piaget, which reached Munari via his son Alberto and daughter-in-law Donata. In particular, Piaget's conviction that play serves as a cognitive laboratory within which children develop the skills by means of which they relate to and comprehend the world. Children enjoy playing because it is through play—initially with objects, later, with abstract symbols—that they exercise control and establish their ability to engage in moral and social reasoning. In the universe of play, it is restrictions and rules, self-imposed or fashioned by educators, that free children up to learn to set and accomplish their goals, to structure their world, and to shape their interactions with one another.[iv]

There are also (unacknowledged) debts to a variety of other sources. Foremost among these to Gianni Rodari, whose *The Grammar of Fantasy—An Introduction to the Art of Inventing Stories* had appeared in 1973, only four years before the publication of *Fantasy*. Munari and Rodari were collaborators. The former illustrated and designed covers for numerous of the latter's children's stories, among them the 1962 *Telephone Fables* (*Favole al telefono*) and 1964 *The Book of Errors* (*Il libro degli errori*). The author of an outstanding corpus of children's literature, Rodari was, at heart, a storyteller, and the "grammatical" structures that most engage his attention are narratological:

> ... [the book is not] an attempt to establish a "fantastics" with rules ready to be taught and studied in school like geometry. Nor is it a complete theory of the imagination and invention, for which more muscle power and someone less ignorant than me would be necessary. Moreover, the book is not even an "essay." In fact, I really do not know what it is. It talks about some ways of inventing stories for children and helping children to invent their own stories. But who knows how many other ways could be found and described? Here I deal only with invention via words and try to suggest, without going too deeply into the matter, that the techniques can easily be transformed into other modes of expression and be used when a story is told by a single teller or by a group.[v]

Alternating between concrete instances of story-telling and references to learned sources (like the late eighteenth-century polymath Novalis, the Russian psychologist Lev Vygotsky, and the American educator Jerome Bruner), *The Grammar of Fantasy* sketches out an anthropology of imaginative play. But whereas Munari is firmly anchored in the visual realm, Rodari's attention is just as firmly anchored in practices of literary invention: in the techniques and strategies for generating stories, performing them, and translating them across media. Despite this core divergence, in many ways *The Grammar of Fantasy* can be said to be the narratological double of Munari's *Fantasy*.

However productive, speculation regarding "sources" can prove misleading in the case of a book as idiosyncratic as *Fantasy*. That's because Munari was a famously prolific, lightning-quick study capable of absorbing and making his own ideas that were, so to speak, "in the air" (so much so that some designer peers in Milan are said to have hidden their work whenever Munari visited, out of fear that he might return the next morning with his own improved version). Always close to the publishing industry, Munari read widely. Sometimes he read deeply. On the whole, however, his sources of inspiration are more experiential or observational than bookish or textual. A case in point is the recurring presence of Japanese references—from bonsai trees to Zen gardens to origami—in the book, the result of his visits to Japan in the 1960s. On the occasion of his first trip (in 1960), Munari traveled to Tokyo for an exhibition of polarized light projections at the National Museum of Modern Art. On the second (in 1965), he presented his kinetic *Tetracono* sculpture, installed a Zen fountain of his own devising (the "five drop fountain") in the Isetan department store, and performed a demonstration of his "original xerographies," consolidating ties to a circle of prominent figures like the surrealist poet Shuzo Takiguchi and the designer Sori Yanagi with which he would remain in contact for another decade.

Likewise, the multiple references in *Fantasy* to the American cinema, from the comedies of the silent-film era (Lawrence Semon, Buster Keaton, Charlie Chaplin) to now mostly forgotten midcentury sci-fi blockbusters like *Tarantula*, *The Incredible Shrinking Man*, *Fantastic Voyage*, and *The Alligator People*, reflects not book learning but the eclecticism of Munari's personal predilections.

Is there a method here? Yes, but it isn't methodical in any narrow sense of the word. Perhaps the (non-) conclusion to *Fantasy* best captures the playful and practical spirit of Munari's overall approach. No summing up of the state of the argument, no gestures of closure, prepare the reader for the book's conclusion. Instead, the end arrives in the form of an anecdote and an exercise. The anecdote demonstrates how a cluster of stains on a wall can give birth to an imaginary museum and a concatenation of related adventures. The exercise shows how a universe of geometries can be generated from within a single leaf. Variations on this operation are at once "personal and infinite" (215) we are assured. "More than a billion combinations are possible" (216).

The book of *Fantasy* is left open by design. For future completion.

i   Among the many instances of such Munarian autobiographies as inventories is the one that prefaces his anthology of short writings *Verbale scritto* (Genoa: Il melangolo, 1992). The formula was repeated in accounts of his work in periodicals and on exhibition posters, among other places.

ii The original edition was *Fantasia* (Rome: Laterza, 1977). The present edition meticulously follows the layout, format, and sequence of the first edition.

iii Quoted from *Xerografia: Documentazione sull'uso creativo delle macchine Rank Xerox* (Milan: Rank Xerox, 1970), 24. Unless otherwise indicated, all translations are my own.

iv Piaget's theories are articulated in such influential books as *The Child's Construction of Reality* (1955), *Play, Dreams, and Imitation in Childhood* (1962) and *The Moral Judgment of the Child* (1966). For useful summing up of the place of Piaget within the broader stream of ideas regarding play, childhood development, and education see Thomas S. Henricks, "Play Studies: A Brief History," *American Journal of Play* 12, vol. 2 (Winter 2020): 117–55.

v   *The Grammar of Fantasy*, trans. Jack Zipes (New York: Teachers and Writers Collective, 1996), 3. The original edition of *Grammatica della fantasia* was published in 1973 by Einaudi.

Production Notes

This book—the first English translation of Bruno Munari's
Fantasia—was produced with the intention of faithfully
capturing the spirit of the original Italian edition.
The design of that book has an energy and flow that
we have sought to preserve and extend. Some design
details may appear idiosyncratic to the contemporary
eye, such as a relatively loose approach to page
construction, a range of image quality, typesetting
particulars such as visibly wide word-spacing, a variety
of approaches to paragraph breaks, etc. We believe this
facsimile is a lively book that's both of its original time
and far beyond.

The cover is newly designed by IN-FO.CO; the illustration
is from the original book, although we chose not to carry
through that cover layout, templated as it was from a
larger series of books published by Laterza.

Body text for the translation is set in Linotype's digiti-
zation of Simoncini Garamond, designed in the 1950s
by Francesco Simoncini and Wilhelm Bilz, and based
on Jean Jannon's seventeenth-century type designs
(commonly misattributed to Claude Garamond).

The new annotations, essay, and back matter are set in
Forma DJR by David Jonathan Ross and Roger Black,
a recent revival of Forma, originally designed by a group
led by Aldo Novarese and released in 1968.

The cover features the typeface Captured, designed by
Jonathan Maghen of Primary Foundry, inspired by credit
card capture technology developed in 1960 by IBM.

—Adam Michaels

Bruno Munari: Fantasy
is published by
Inventory Press
2305 Hyperion Ave
Los Angeles, CA 90027
inventorypress.com

Translation
Jeffrey Schnapp

Copyediting and Proofreading
Eugenia Bell

Design and Facsimile Production
IN-FO.CO (Adam Michaels, Shannon Harvey, James Blue,
Clara Chirila-Rus), Matt Harvey, Thomas Bollier

Printed and bound in the US by Sheridan

ISBN: 978-1-941753-70-5
LCCN: 2024944592

Distributed by
ARTBOOK | D.A.P.
75 Broad St, Suite 630
New York, NY 10004
artbook.com